Exciting accounts of the teams that reached the world championships of football and of the games in which they won or lost the title. John Devaney provides glimpses of Vince Lombardi, Joe Namath, Bart Starr, Johnny Unitas and many others as they compete for victory in America's biggest sporting event— the Super Bowl!

SUPER BOWL!

by John Devaney

Illustrated with photographs

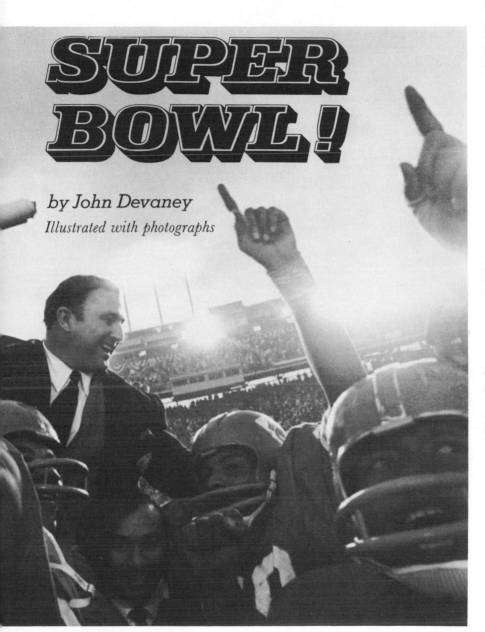

RANDOM HOUSE
NEW YORK

for my father

For a great deal of help in the preparation of this book, I would like to thank Joe Browne and other members of the National Football League office in New York.

CONTENTS

SUPER BOWL!

Lamar Hunt, president of the Kansas City Chiefs.

The Beginning

THE LITTLE GIRL threw her special rubber ball against the wall. The ball bounced off the wall, bounding crazily around the room.

The girl turned to her father. "This is my super ball," she said, laughing.

A few weeks later her father, Lamar Hunt, the millionaire owner of the Kansas City Chiefs, was at a meeting of owners of American Football League and National Football League teams. They were discussing a game long dreamed of by fans. This game, between the best team in the AFL and the best team in the NFL, would be the world series of football.

"How about calling it the World Championship Game?" said one.

"How about calling it The Big One?" said another.

Lamar Hunt frowned, recalling what his daughter had called the ball of silly putty.

"I have a suggestion," he said to the other men. "Let's call it the Super Bowl."

SUPER
BOWL I

Bart Starr, quarterback of the Green Bay Packers.

The Fall of the Hammer

"IT'S BEEN a war of words for seven years. Now it's nice to have the war on grass where it belongs."

Speaking was Hank Stram, the cherubic-faced coach of the Kansas City Chiefs. The seven-year war of words had involved players, fans and writers in many hot arguments between 1961 and 1967. In one camp they were saying things like this: "The Packers would mop up the best team in the AFL."

The other camp answered, "The Buffalo Bills, with that big fullback Cookie Gilchrist, they could murder any team in the NFL."

The war had started when the American Football League was organized in 1960. The AFL recruited players who had not been able to play regularly, or at all, in the older, well-established National Football League. The new league also tried to convince college stars to pass up NFL offers and sign with an AFL team. It did get a few, notably LSU's bruising ball carrier and Heisman Trophy winner, Billy Cannon. But for the most part the league was made

7

up of players who, as one writer said, "were has-
beens or never-wases."

Slowly, though, the league improved year after
year, luring such college stars as Joe Namath, Matt
Snell, E.J. Holub and Mike Garrett. And players
like Kansas City quarterback Len Dawson, who had
been sitting on the bench in the NFL, were playing
with such brilliance that many fans were saying,
"The NFL never gave them a chance to be good."

But the NFL supporters smiled at such state-
ments. "Dawson," they said, "would still be warming a bench in our league." Most people still be-
lieved that the NFL was far superior.

Now the war of words seemed over: the two
leagues, after coming to peace with each other, had
agreed to match the best team in the NFL against
the best team in the AFL. Pro football Commissioner Pete Rozelle wanted to call the game "the
world's championship of football." But Lamar
Hunt's little daughter had helped him to come up
with a catchier name: Super Bowl. And Super Bowl
it would be.

In the AFL the Kansas City Chiefs had defeated
the Buffalo Bills for the 1966 league championship.
As the battered, happy Chiefs filed off the field, the
mammoth 270-pound tackle for the Bills, Jim Duna-
way, shouted at them, "Let's show 'em. Show those
NFL guys what kind of football we play in the
AFL."

That evening, flying back to Kansas City, the
Chiefs talked about how much this Super Bowl

game would mean to them. "I'm glad we're representing the league," said offensive tackle Jim Tyrer, who had been playing for six years in the AFL, almost since its beginning. "You don't know what this means to us. Do you know how it feels to have your ability questioned the way ours was for all those years by the NFL? Now we're within sight of what we wanted for a long time—the chance to prove what we can do."

Little Mike Garrett, an All-League running back despite his fire-hydrant size, nodded as he listened to Tyrer. "I realize how all the AFL veterans feel," he said. "And I know how I feel. I want to show all the people in this country how good this league is. Like all my life they said I was too small. And for years they've been saying this league isn't good enough. I think we'll show them that this league is good enough to play anybody in the NFL—even the big bad Packers."

The big Packers had won the 1966 NFL championship. Never, however, had they won a title game by so scary a margin. In the closing moments, the Packers led 34-27, but the Dallas Cowboys had driven to the Packer two-yard line. But there the tough, gutsy Packer defense held, and for the fourth time in six years the Green Bay Packers were champions of the National Football League.

The Packers were the NFL's best, no doubt about it. Their coach was the famous Vince Lombardi, that rock-like, hard-faced man who treated all his players alike—"like dogs," one of them once said. At quarterback there was Bart Starr, the one they called Bart the Cool, poised and alert in tense situations. The running backs were the bull-like Jim Taylor and Paul Hornung, a clever runner and a hard blocker. Up on the line were tough men like tackle Jerry Kramer and the pass-catching end, Carroll Dale. On defense were hard-nosed types like Dave Robinson, who once said he looked upon opponents the way he would look upon a thief who was sneaking into his house at night. "What would you do to a thief you caught stealing your money?" Robinson said, glowering. "That's the way I treat a man who tries to run by me out there on a football field."

These were tough men and proud men. They were proud of their record, and they knew what the Packer name meant to football fans: the best.

"We will be representing an entire league in the Super Bowl," middle linebacker Ray Nitschke said a few days before the game. "That is, an entire league besides our own team, our own pride, our own winning tradition."

Someone asked Bart Starr if the Packers were thinking about the money they could win in this game—$15,000 for each winning player, compared to $7,500 for each loser. He smiled in his pleasant-mannered way, and said, "Well, naturally you think about the money. But the money is really secondary. A lot of people will find that hard to believe, but it's really true."

The truest feelings of the Packers were expressed by guard Jerry Kramer. "We'll have to go into hiding if we lose," he said. "For years the public has been brought up to believe the AFL was an inferior product. Now, suddenly it's up to us to make good. We'll be labeled the biggest fakes and phonies in the history of pro sports if we lose."

The first Super Bowl was to be played in the huge 100,000-seat Los Angeles Coliseum. Both coaches, Vince Lombardi and Hank Stram, said they were happy to be playing in sunny California instead of frigid Green Bay or windy Kansas City. But Lombardi summed up what both coaches thought about weather and football. "The weather doesn't beat you," Lombardi said, a trace of a smile around his brick of a jaw. "The other team beats you."

The Packers flew to a training camp at Santa Barbara, the Chiefs to one at Long Beach, both not far from Los Angeles. Each team received three game films from the other team. For two weeks, night and day, coaches and players stared at those films, looking for the strengths and weaknesses of the opposition.

The coaches drew up charts outlining how they saw the other team. This is what the Kansas City charts said.

Packers on offense: The running backs are Jim Taylor, who is older now and less likely to break away for the long gain, and Elijah Pitts, young and fast. Pitts, replacing the injured Paul Hornung, is not the blocker that Hornung is, but is more difficult to bring down in the open field. Bart Starr passes more

than he did in recent years, is very accurate (62%
completion rate), rarely is intercepted (only three
times all season). Carroll Dale is a dangerous receiver on deep patterns, and Taylor, Boyd Dowler,
Marv Fleming, and Max McGee run complex short
patterns. Starr's timing with his receivers is excellent; he hits them with passes as they turn away
from a defender and are momentarily free. He is especially good at throwing to his receivers on third-
down-and-short-yardage situations.

Packers on defense: The right side of the line, with
Lionel Aldridge and Henry Jordan, is not big and
the Chiefs plan to attack it with their running game.
The linebackers—Dave Robinson, Ray Nitschke,
Lee Roy Caffey—are among the best in the NFL.
They seldom blitz, dropping back in passing situa-
tions to cover receivers. At the corners Bob Jeter and
Herb Adderley knock down runners and stick with
receivers stride for stride. The deep backs, Tom
Brown and Willie Wood, are competent but not up
to the quality of the cornerbacks.

The Packer charts told the Chiefs' story.

Chiefs on offense: Mike Garrett is a fast running
back who can go through a closing hole quicker
than an eye-blink. The other back, Curtis McClinton, is an excellent blocker but an ordinary runner.
Quarterback Len Dawson has to have time to
throw. He will roll out behind a moving shield of

Mike Garrett of the Chiefs carries the ball against
Green Bay.

blockers to get more time to find a receiver. The Chief receivers are their strongest asset. Flanker Otis Taylor is fast and elusive, has remarkable hands and jumping ability, and likes to go deep. Split end Chris Burford is not especially fast, but can cut to the sideline exceptionally well for the short five-yard pass. Fred Arbanas is an excellent blocker at tight end and is good at catching passes over the middle in heavy traffic.

Chiefs on defense: The front line is huge, with people like Buck Buchanan (6-foot-7, 286 pounds), Jerry Mays (6-foot-4, 255), and Andy Rice (6-foot-2, 268). But their quickness is questionable. The three linebackers are Bobby Bell, one of the best in the game, Sherrill Headrick, and E.J. Holub. Holub has been slowed by injuries and can be beaten on short passes to a cutting halfback. Unlike most AFL teams, the Chiefs do not blitz too often. The cornerbacks, Fred (The Hammer) Williamson and Willie Mitchell, are the weak points in the Kansas City defense, and both can be exploited for short passes. They will need help from the deep backs, Johnny Robinson and Bobby Hunt, two of the best in the AFL at intercepting passes.

The Packer coach clicked off the projector and flipped the switch, lighting the room. He and the other coaches had been watching the Chiefs in a game against Buffalo. Now they were discussing the Kansas City defense.

"That stacked defense of theirs looks a little like

Detroit's," one coach said. They had also noticed that the Chiefs did a lot of unusual things on defense. It would be difficult to run against them. But they wouldn't be able to get a very good rush on the passer because their men lined up one man behind the other. Starr should be able to pass against them and they would be especially vulnerable to short passes because their secondary played very loose, hanging back.

Some 100 miles south, in Long Beach, the Chiefs were sitting in hotel rooms, watching game films of the Packers. They watched Starr drop back to throw a pass. Safetyman Johnny Robinson was worried about Starr. "I've never seen that guy throw a bad pass in the three films we've seen," he said. "He places the ball at just the right spot where the receiver has the advantage."

Len Dawson was in an adjoining room conferring with Hank Stram. Dawson usually spoke in a low voice, almost a mumble. His eyes were as pale as marbles. When he was angry with someone, he simply stared at the offender. "When Lenny gives you The Look," said one Chief, "you never forget it."

Len was studying a book of Chief plays. He and coach Stram had decided not to change very much on offense. They planned to use a lot of play-action passes. Dawson would fake handing off the ball to one of the running backs, Garrett in particular. Then after the fake, he would go back to pass and have a little more time while the Packers recovered.

Dawson would be looking to pass to Chris Burford especially. Burford was the Chiefs' split end. The Packer secondary would be watching flanker Otis Taylor, who had led the AFL during the season in yards gained per catch, averaging 22 yards for each reception. Shortly before the game Packer cornerback Herb Adderley, who would be covering Taylor, said, "Otis is in the same class as the top NFL receivers. I'll be concentrating on him. But I don't intend to change my game. I'll play the same as I have the last five years. I'll play him as close as I can—inside his shirt if I have to."

Herb stared at the floor a moment, "A cornerback has to concentrate on one man. Most cornerbacks get beaten on a pass for a touchdown because they look into the backfield at the fakes. The secret is, just watch your man and don't follow the play action."

The clock was ticking off the final 24 hours before what newspapers were calling "The Game." Some of the players began to show their emotions as they waited for the game.

"I've got to talk about the game to stay relaxed," E.J. Holub was telling a friend on the eve of the game. "If I don't, the palms of my hands sweat. I get to be a nervous wreck. But if I talk about the game, I don't let myself get too psyched up."

One player who was already psyched up was Fred Williamson, a Chief cornerback who called himself The Hammer. "I am the greatest," The Hammer was telling a group of newspapermen one day. "I am going to drop The Hammer on Green Bay."

He pointed to his upper arm and made a karate-like chopping motion with it. "This is The Hammer," he said. "Whenever I hit them with The Hammer, I make it hurt."

"You sound like Cassius Clay," one writer said.

Williamson grinned. He didn't mind at all being compared to the fighter. "When I first started playing defense," he told the writers, "I knew the receiver would have a psychological advantage. He knows where he is going. So, being the intelligent person that I am, it was very easy to calculate a method for overcoming this. I don't fight them, I intimidate them."

He pointed again to his muscular arms. "I don't know how many helmets The Hammer has busted. At least 30 so far. I'll be playing Carroll Dale on Sunday and he had better watch out for The Hammer."

The Chiefs' Jim Tyrer overheard The Hammer. "A lot of us don't like the way The Hammer plays," Tyrer said. "But he does make a lot of big plays for us. In the AFL championship game he hit a receiver so hard he fumbled the ball. We recovered, and that set up our final touchdown."

A writer phoned Carroll Dale and told him about The Hammer's threats. Dale laughed. "It will be interesting," Dale said, "to see if he plays as well as he talks."

January 15th, 1967, dawned bright in Los Angeles. The sun burned down on the Coliseum

through a soft haze, and the temperature was in the 70s. More than 60,000 people were on hand for the game. The stands were splotched with colors—the red Chief banners, the green Packer pennants. Most of the fans were for the Chiefs. "I'm rooting for Kansas City," said one Los Angeles man, "because Mike Garrett plays for the Chiefs and he used to play here at USC."

"Rooting for Green Bay," his friend said, "is like rooting for an IBM machine."

That machine, though, was the heavy favorite to win. One writer had predicted that the final score would be Green Bay 84, Kansas City 0. Others, more serious, forecast a Green Bay victory by two to four touchdowns. Only a brave few picked the Chiefs. The NFL's Packers, declared the writers, had more experience and talent.

"I know we're the underdogs," the Chiefs' Sherrill Headrick told his teammates after they had finished their limbering-up exercises on the field. "But let's go out and play tough. This game is the biggest thing that's ever happened in sports, and this is our chance to be remembered because we played well in it."

At one end of the field the Packers were kicking and throwing an NFL ball. At the other end the Chiefs were kicking and throwing an AFL ball. When the Packers were on offense, they would use

Vince Lombardi kneels on the sideline as Super Bowl I begins.

the NFL ball. When the Chiefs were on offense, the officials would put an AFL ball into play.

The time was 1:16 p.m., the sun now so warm that some men had taken off their jackets and were watching in shirtsleeves. The crowd was standing, a roar swelling upward as the two teams lined up facing each other for the opening kickoff, the Packers in green and gold jerseys, the Chiefs in white jerseys with red numerals. The Chiefs' Fletcher (Duck) Smith ran forward and kicked the ball. It soared some 50 yards downfield to the Packer 5-yard line and the first Super Bowl game had begun. The Packers' kickoff team returned the ball 20 yards.

The ball sat on the tufted grass at the Green Bay 25. Cautiously testing, Starr jabbed three running plays into the midsection of the Chiefs' line, the third jab for a first down. On the next series he tried out his passing attack. As Starr stepped back to pass, the big Chief line tore through his blocking. Twice the Chiefs flattened Starr for losses. With fourth and 25 to go from their 27, the Packers punted.

The Chiefs' offense took possession of the ball at their 37. Immediately Dawson tested the Packers' pass defense, sending Otis Taylor deep. He saw Herb Adderley running right with Otis, almost inside his shirt, as he had threatened. Dawson turned to look for Chris Burford, cutting toward the side-line. He threw to Burford, who caught the ball, but out of bounds.

Twice more Dawson angled passes to Burford cutting toward the sidelines in what the receivers call an "out" pattern. He completed one pass to Burford for a first down on the Green Bay 48. But here the Packer defense stiffened, and the Chiefs had to punt, the Packers returning the ball to their own 20.

Starr, working on a game plan that called for more passing than running against the Chiefs' stacked defense, threw over the middle to Marv Fleming for a first down. Again Starr called for a pass. The big Chief linemen crashed through his blockers. Starr ducked under a swinging white-shirted arm, straightened, then coolly arched a pass that Elijah Pitts caught on the run at the Kansas City 44, where he was knocked down by two Chiefs.

A running play gained five yards. In the huddle Starr stared at the right side of the Chiefs' defense. This area was usually well protected by the Chiefs' Johnny Robinson, an All-Star safetyman. But Starr —and the Green Bay coaches, who were watching from atop the stadium—had seen something: Robinson was busy running to the Chiefs' left side to help out Fred (The Hammer) Williamson, who was turning out not to be The Greatest on pass coverage. With Robinson gone, Willie Mitchell was the only defender in the area. Starr was hoping to catch Mitchell making a mistake that would leave a Packer open.

First he threw a pass to Carroll Dale on the left side, completing the pass. As expected, Johnny Robinson vacated the right side to help out on the left.

It was third down and three yards to go from the

Chiefs' 37. Starr called for another pass. On the snap, split end Max McGee, a wily veteran, cut toward Mitchell. Again, Mitchell was alone, Robinson having left the area. And Mitchell made the mistake that Starr wanted to see: as McGee cut, Mitchell turned the wrong way, giving McGee a split-second to get ahead of him. Starr whipped a pass that zipped over Mitchell's helmet. McGee reached for the ball. It struck his hand and bounded upward into the air. McGee snatched at it, grabbing it with both hands at the Kansas City 19, and dashed into the end zone with Mitchell chasing him from behind. Don Chandler kicked the extra point and the Packers led 7-0.

The Packers still led by that one touchdown as the second quarter began. With the ball on his 34, Dawson began to use more of the play-action passes that were a major part of the Chiefs' game plan. His faked handoffs to the runners seemed to confuse and immobilize the Packer defense. The Packers were not rushing forward on passes, and on runs they were letting the ball carriers plunge by. They were sticking out hands and arms to trip up the runners instead of smacking them down with their bodies. In one huddle a Packer tackle, Ron Kostelnik, said to a teammate: "I've never seen so much play-action stuff in one game."

From his own 34, Dawson threw a pass to little

Max McGee juggles Bart Starr's pass. He finally caught it and scored on the play.

Mike Garrett on the Green Bay 49. On the next play he handed off to halfback Bert Coan who dashed three yards to the 46. Again, Dawson dashed back as if to pass but he handed off to Curt McClinton on a fullback draw play, and burly Curt plowed six yards to the 40. Coan broke through the left side for two yards and the first down at the 38.

On the next play Dawson faked handing off to Coan, stepped back and lined a pass to Otis Taylor, who was running down the left sideline. Taylor caught the ball over his shoulder and was knocked out of bounds at the Packer 7.

Dawson did not give the Packer defense a chance to get its breath. He told McClinton to run a slanting pattern over the middle. Dawson stepped back and fired a pass into McClinton's arms at the goal line. The brawny fullback thundered into the end zone for the touchdown. With the crowd still roaring, Tommy Mercer kicked the extra-point and the Chiefs and the Packers were tied 7-7.

The Packers returned the kickoff to their 27. With third and one on his own 36, Starr tried a play that had made Johnny Unitas famous at Baltimore. He faked handing off to a runner plunging into the line. The defense rushed up to stop the short gain. Then Starr cocked his arm and arched a long pass. Carroll Dale was running down the middle, shooting by the Chiefs who rushed up to stop the plunging back. He caught the ball all alone at the Chiefs' 33 and ran untouched into the end zone. But as he crossed the goal line, an official's flag lay on the grass upfield.

The official had detected an illegal move by a Packer lineman just before the snap. The ball was brought back, the touchdown nullified, and now it was third and six for Starr from the 31.

Not at all ruffled, Bart ran back and completed a pass to Max McGee. First down on the Green Bay 42.

A minute later, after two unsuccessful passes, Starr faced another third-down situation—third and 10 from the 42. He had to complete this pass or give up the ball. Again he stepped back and completed the pass, zipping the ball into Carroll Dale's hands at the Kansas City 43.

Two running plays gained five yards. Again it was that agonizing time for a quarterback—third down and substantial yardage to go. Starr called for a pass. As he ran back, he saw Marv Fleming open for a moment between Chief defenders Johnny Robinson and Willie Mitchell. He threadneedled the pass between the two defenders. Fleming caught the ball and was dropped at the 27 for a first down.

A minute later Bart faced another critical third-down play: third and seven to go from the 24. The Chiefs, knowing he would be passing, smashed into Starr's cup of blockers, but this time the blockers held their ground. Starr saw Pitts crossing the middle, chased by the slower E.J. Holub. Starr lobbed a pass that Pitts caught at the 14, where he was knocked down by Holub.

In the huddle Starr called for that granddaddy of Packer plays: the power sweep. On the snap the two guards, Jerry Kramer and Fuzzy Thurston, pulled backward out of the line and dashed to the left. Starr handed off to fullback Jim Taylor who followed a moving wave of green-shirted blockers, led by the two guards. That green wave rolled over the white-shirted Chiefs and swept into the end zone, Taylor following with the ball. Don Chandler kicked the extra point and the Packers led 14-7.

The Green Bay fans, sitting in the Coliseum or watching TV across the country, settled back. "The good old power sweep," they were saying with smug smiles. "We showed 'em who's the boss. Now we'll run 'em off the field."

Instead, the underdog Chiefs scrapped back. From his own 26, with time running out in the half, Dawson darted short, quick passes to Chris Burford, Fred Arbanas and Mike Garrett, the receivers slanting across the middle from the left or right sides. And by faking handoffs before passing, he kept the Packer rushers frozen, not knowing whether the play was a run or a pass. With time to look for his receivers, he completed one pass after another. From the sideline Lombardi screamed, "Get 'em! get 'em!" But the Packer defense could not stop the Chief receivers. With only 1:37 remaining in the first half, Dawson threw a third-down pass complete to Garrett over the middle at the Green Bay 24.

Fourth down and two yards to go. In from the Chief bench ran Tommy Mercer, the field-goal kicker. Dawson took the snap from the center, placed down the ball, and Mercer kicked it through the uprights. The Chiefs now trailed, 14-10. As the gun barked, ending the first half, millions of people across the country were wondering: were they about to see one of the great upsets of sports history?

The Packers trotted off the field. As Doug Hart, a substitute defensive back said later, "We went into the game feeling we would win, but at halftime we realized we had a tough game on our hands."

In the Packer dressing room the players flopped on the floor, munching on oranges. The defense sat on one side of the room, the offense on the other, listening to their coaches. Lombardi walked over to the defense. "Stop grabbing and start tackling," he roared at the defensive team.

The players knew well what Lombardi meant. In the first half they had played cautiously, concerned that Dawson might spring a trick on them. They had been thinking too much and hitting not enough. "Let's go out there and start knocking people down," Ray Nitschke shouted.

The Chiefs walked out of their dressing room for the start of the second half feeling an inner confidence they had not felt before the game. They had met the glorified Green Bay machine and matched it, almost point for point, for 30 minutes. This machine could be stopped, it could be beaten.

The Packers huddled near their bench. "What we need," defensive back Willie Wood said to another player, "is the one big play to wake us up."

The big play was coming—for the Packers and Willie Wood.

The Chiefs took the kickoff and began to march—starting the second half as they had ended the first half, on the move with the ball. Dawson rolled out for 15 yards. McClinton burst up the middle, Garrett slashed off-tackle, and now the Chiefs had the ball on their own 49, third down and five to go.

In the Chief huddle Dawson called for a pass to Fred Arbanas on the left sideline. In the Packer huddle Ray Nitschke called for something the Packers use no more than once or twice a game: the blitz. Instead of dropping back to cover the receivers, two linebackers would charge across the line at the quarterback. They hoped to knock him down before he could toss a pass to a receiver in the area they had left uncovered. That, of course, was the risk of a blitz: that a receiver would catch a pass in the uncovered area and go all the way for a touchdown.

The two teams lined up. Dawson hut-hutted the signals. He looked at Lee Roy Caffey and Dave Robinson, the two outside Packer linebackers. They were leaning forward, but Dawson did not read blitz.

He took the center's snap, saw the two linebackers converging up the middle toward him, and heard the frantic shouts of the blockers around him, "Blitz! Blitz! Blitz!"

Dawson darted out of the pocket and to his right, looking for Arbanas. Lee Roy Caffey rushed toward him. Dawson leaned back to throw and Caffey hit him. The ball flew out of Dawson's hand in a towering arc.

Willie Wood, running near Arbanas, saw the ball arching toward him. "It's going to be short," Wood thought. He slipped away from Arbanas, running toward the ball.

The ball seemed to be hanging in the blue sky. "Won't it ever come down?" Willie thought, watching, hands stretched forward toward the ball. He thought he heard footsteps—was Arbanas coming back to try to grab the pass?

The ball dropped into Wood's arms. He raced down the sideline—past the 40, the 30, the 20, the 10. The speedy Mike Garrett caught Wood from behind and knocked him down at the Kansas City 5.

Wood got up and ran to the Packer bench. "That's the big play, that's what we needed," a Packer yelled at Willie. Wood grinned.

Bart Starr did not waste a moment before taking advantage of the opportunity. He handed off to Elijah Pitts, who plowed over left tackle and bounded into the end zone for the touchdown.

The Packers now led 21-10, and a lot of that confidence drained out of the Chiefs. Now they had to play catch-up football. They had to pass, and the Packers knew they had to pass. No longer could Dawson keep them off-balance with those play-action passes that froze the Green Bay defense. Each time Dawson dashed back to pass, the Green Bay line—and, often, blitzing linebackers—converged on

The Packers' Elijah Pitts crosses the goal line for a Green Bay touchdown. ➡

him, blocking his view or knocking him down. Once Lee Roy Caffey and Willie Davis dumped him for a 14-yard loss. On the next play Ron Kostelnik and Davis buried him for an 11-yard loss.

Dawson looked for Otis Taylor, hoping to throw the long touchdown "bomb." But Herb Adderley was sticking tight to Taylor, and whenever Dawson threw to Taylor, Adderley was there to bat the pass away. In the entire fourth period Dawson completed only one pass to Taylor, good for only four yards.

Now the Packers were on the march again, smashing from their own 44 to the Chiefs' 13. From there Starr threw another line-drive pass at Max McGee. Again, McGee slipped by Mitchell, turned and saw the ball streaking toward him. The ball hit McGee's hands again and bounced up into the air. Again, he grabbed the ball, held it and raced down the middle into the end zone. The Packers led 28-10.

Still the Packers were not through. Midway through the fourth period they marched again, driving from their own 20 into the Chiefs' end zone, Elijah Pitts scoring from the 1. Now the score was Green Bay 35, Kansas City 10. Both coaches sent in their subs to run out the clock.

The gun sounded, ending the game. The Packers had won 35-10. The Packers roared into their dressing room, clapping each other on the back. Lombardi's raw voice cut through the bedlam, demanding silence. He told the players they had much to be thankful for: they had won, no one had been seriously hurt. Then he knelt and led the players in saying the Lord's Prayer.

The press flooded into the room. Al Silverman, the editor of *Sport* magazine, walked over to Starr and presented him with a set of keys. Starr had won a sports car for being the game's most valuable player. Bart had completed 16 of 23 passes, good for 250 yards and two touchdowns. Those statistics did not tell the full measure of his contribution to the victory. Seven times he had stepped back to pass on third down, knowing he had to complete the pass or give up the ball. Five times he completed the do-or-die pass (the sixth time he was knocked down and the seventh time the receiver dropped the pass). By comparison, Dawson tried to pass nine times on third down and threw only one completion.

"That was where they won the game," Chief coach Hank Stram said in the loser's clubhouse. "It was in Starr's ability—it was almost uncanny—to come up with the successful third-down play. Starr was the single difference between the two teams."

The Packers thought they were better in every department. "The Chiefs are a good team," said Vince Lombardi, "but they don't compare with the teams in the NFL. Dallas is a better team and so are several others."

Fred (The Hammer) Williamson was sitting on a stool in the Chiefs' locker room, holding an aching head. Late in the game a Packer guard, Gale Gillingham, had run into him, knocking him out. The Hammer had not fallen on the Packers, as he had

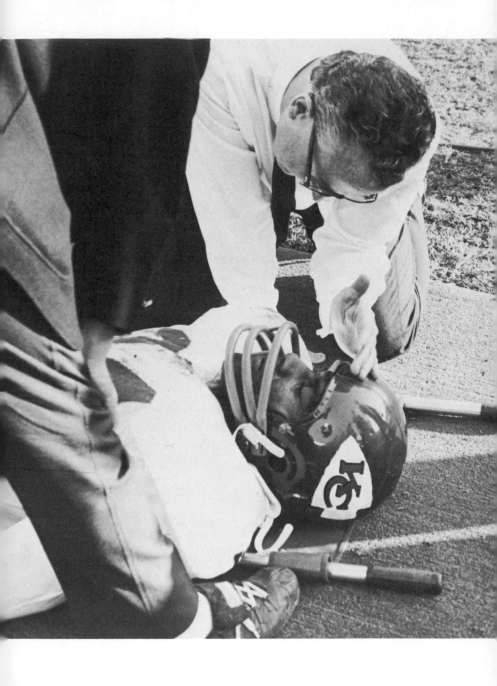

predicted. Instead, another hammer, Gale Gillingham, had fallen on Williamson.

But The Hammer was still talking. "They got all the breaks," he said loudly. "If we played them tomorrow, we could beat them."

The Packers laughed when they heard what Williamson had said. "Same old Hammer," one said, scornfully.

One Packer said he thought the Atlanta Falcons, a last-place NFL team, could beat the Chiefs. But Lance Alworth, an AFL player for San Diego, who had watched the game, said: "The day will come when an AFL team will beat an NFL team."

The first Super Bowl had come and gone, but the war of words went on.

Fred (The Hammer) Williamson is placed on a stretcher after being knocked out by the Packers' Gale Gillingham.

SUPER BOWL I
(Played in Los Angeles Coliseum,
January 15, 1967)

Scoring by quarters:

	1	2	3	4	Totals
Kansas City Chiefs	0	10	0	0	10
Green Bay Packers	7	7	14	7	35

Scoring plays:

Team	Period	Elapsed Time	Scoring Plays	Packers	Chiefs
Packers	1	8:56	McGee, 37-yd. pass from Starr	6	0
			Chandler, conversion (kick)	7	0
Chiefs	2	4:20	McClinton, 7-yd. pass from Dawson	7	6
			Mercer, conversion (kick)	7	7
Packers	2	10:23	Taylor, 14-yd. run	13	7
			Chandler, conversion (kick)	14	7
Chiefs	2	14:06	Mercer, 31-yd. field goal	14	10
Packers	3	2:27	Pitts, 5-yd. run	20	10
			Chandler, conversion (kick)	21	10
Packers	3	14:09	McGee, 13-yd. pass from Starr	27	10
			Chandler, conversion (kick)	28	10
Packers	4	8:25	Pitts, 1-yd. run	34	10
			Chandler, conversion (kick)	35	10

Team Statistics

	Green Bay	Kansas City
Score....................	35	10
Touchdowns..............	5	1
P.A.T....................	5	1
Kick (A-M)............	5-5	1-1
Field Goals (A-M)..........	0-0	1-2
First Downs...............	21	17
Rushing................	10	4
Passing................	11	12
Penalty................	0	1
Total Offense.............	358	239
Rushing................	130	72
Passing................	228	167
Passing		
Attempts...............	24	32
Completions............	16	17
Had Intercepted........	1	1
Yards Gained...........	228	167
Touchdowns.............	2	0
Punting		
Number................	4	7
Yards.................,	173	317
Average................	43.3	43.3
Punt Returns		
Number................	4	3
Yards.................	23	19
Average................	5.8	6.3
Kickoff Returns		
Number................	3	6
Yards.................	65	130
Average................	21.6	21.6
Penalties		
Number................	4	4
Yards.................	40	26

A Last Hurrah for Max and Vince

FIVE OF THE OAKLAND RAIDERS were lounging on the beds and chairs in their hotel room in Boca Raton, Florida, a few hours by car from Miami. Super Bowl II was to be played in Miami's Orange Bowl in three days. Sitting near each other were Gene Upshaw, a 22-year-old giant of a guard, 6-foot-5 and 265 pounds, and Dave Kocourek, a veteran tight end who had played in six AFL championship games.

Upshaw was a rookie. "You know," he was saying, "it's going to feel strange playing against the Green Bay Packers on Sunday. I've been reading about those guys—Starr and Dowler and Jordan and the rest—since I was in junior high school. Now I'm playing against them. It will be almost like playing against your own father."

Kocourek smiled. "We can beat them," he said.

Coach Lombardi talks to Bart Starr (right) during Super Bowl II.

41

"I watched them last year in the Super Bowl against Kansas City. The Chiefs did all right for the first half against the Packers. But when they got behind they discarded the things they had been doing successfully. Even when they got behind they should have stuck to their game plan. Instead they became desperate and began throwing the bomb. It won't happen this time. This team is too solid to deviate from its game plan that much."

The Raiders were a young team. They had no superstar to gain the headlines, yet they had surprised the AFL in 1967. They had won 13 of their 14 games. Only a few years earlier they had won only three games over a two-year period. The team had been improved dramatically by general manager Al Davis' shrewd trades and young coach Johnny Rauch's equally shrewd tactics. In the 1967 AFL championship game the Raiders demolished Houston, 40-7. Their quarterback, Daryle Lamonica, tossed two touchdown passes. And the team's "old man," No. 2 quarterback George Blanda, who had started out with the Chicago Bears way back in 1949, kicked four field goals. Now Lamonica was leading this young Raider team into the Super Bowl against the National Football League's tested, veteran Green Bay Packers.

Green Bay had struggled painfully along the road to its second straight Super Bowl. Their young running backs, Donny Anderson and Jim Grabowski, who had replaced the traded Jim Taylor and the retired Paul Hornung, had been hurt. Their fleet defensive back, Herb Adderley, had split a muscle in his arm. He continued to play but often he could not lift his arm to bat down a pass.

"How can you keep on playing?" someone asked him.

"You know what Mr. Lombardi says," Herb answered. "He says you have to play with the small hurts."

The Packers had won only 9 of 14 games in 1967, but they had won their division title. In the playoff for the Western Conference championship they had been the underdogs against a huge Ram team that had defeated them 27-24 earlier in the season. The Rams had lost only once all season and seemed unbeatable. But Green Bay's tigers overcame the mountainous Ram linemen in the playoff to win the western title, 28-7.

Then, on frigid Lambeau Field in Green Bay, with the temperature an icy 13 degrees below zero, the Packers clashed with the Dallas Cowboys for the NFL championship. They were losing 17-14. With only 13 seconds left, they were on the Cowboys' 1-foot-line. They might have kicked an almost certain field goal to tie the game and send it into sudden death overtime. But Bart Starr and the Packers disdained going for a tying field goal. They went for broke. Bart Starr called his own number and dived over the line for the winning touchdown. For the third straight year the Packers were NFL champions and on their way to the blessed warmth of Miami and Super Bowl II.

Someone once asked Lombardi to explain the success of the Packers. "We have a great love for one another," Lombardi said.

"It's true," linebacker Dave Robinson once said. "I know it seems strange to say that a bunch of grown men are in love with one another, and maybe love isn't the right word. But we have great respect and admiration for one another. We don't want to let any one of us down. So we are always playing as hard as we can to win."

In talking about the close-knit unity of the Packers, guard Jerry Kramer liked to talk about Doug Hart, a defensive back who had been a starter in 1965 and then lost his position to Bob Jeter. "He should be upset," Kramer wrote in his book, *Instant Replay.* "He should be sulking or demanding to be traded. Right? Wrong. Not here. He's one of the best men we have on our special units. He hustles harder than anybody on the club."

Kramer also talked about Fuzzy Thurston in the book. The veteran Fuzzy had been replaced at left guard by rookie Gale Gillingham. "I'm sure it hurt Fuzzy," Kramer wrote. "I'm sure he felt bad about losing his job. But he sat behind Gilly in every movie, he talked with him, he coached him, he was just like a big brother. He did everything he could to make Gilly a better ballplayer. This is why we win, I guess."

The Packers trained at a baseball stadium in Fort Lauderdale, about an hour's drive from Miami. One morning, as they grouped around him on the grass to do their calisthenics, Lombardi addressed his team. "This is the most important game of your lives," he told them. "It's certainly the most important of my life."

Later, in the dressing room, the Packers talked about what Lombardi had said. What did he mean, the most important game of his life? Maybe the rumors were true that Lombardi, both head coach and general manager of the Packers, would retire as coach and become a full-time general manager after the game.

That night Jerry Kramer and Bart Starr ate supper together. Starr said he thought that Lombardi would announce his retirement after the Super Bowl. Inwardly, Jerry Kramer decided he wanted to play this game as perfectly as he could—this crucial last game he would be playing for Coach Vince Lombardi.

No two Packers were closer to each other than running back Paul Hornung and the pass-catching end, Max McGee. They roomed together on the road. Since both were bachelors, they went together to parties and enjoyed the same good times between games. Often the two of them sneaked out of their hotel room after Lombardi's curfew hour to have a good time at a party.

Now the happy pair was split. Hornung had retired after the 1966 season. But before the second Super Bowl the blond, good-humored Hornung showed up at the team's motel driving a multi-colored sports car. The Packers gathered around their old teammate to welcome him.

"I had a dream the other night that I came by and sneaked Max McGee out after hours," he told them. "Vinnie found out about it and darned if he didn't fine me five thousand bucks, even though I wasn't with the team any longer. The thing that woke me up was that I dreamed I paid the fine."

Now the rumor was that Max McGee would be following his old roommate into retirement. Someone asked him if he really meant to retire. He had threatened to quit before.

"I really do," Max said. "Not even the coach can talk me out of it this time. I am going into the restaurant business and the only bruises I am going to get from now on will be whenever a waiter drops a stack of dishes on me." He laughed.

Then he frowned. "After this year a lot of the old guys will be gone." He looked around the locker room. "They say the coach is going to retire and I suppose Fuzzy and maybe Jerry Kramer will quit. In this game you're going to see the last of a lot of the old Packers."

The Raiders were hoping for a good game from their 26-year-old leader and quarterback, Daryle Lamonica, a quiet, confident passer who had been

The Raiders' young quarterback Daryle Lamonica
darts back to pass.

the best in the AFL in 1967. For four years, Lamonica, a former Notre Dame star, had sat on the bench in Buffalo, behind regular quarterback Jack Kemp. Oakland general manager Al Davis saw talent in Lamonica and obtained him in a trade, helping to turn the Raiders' fortunes for the better.

Lamonica showed his talent in a big game against San Diego in 1967. Oakland led 10-7 early in the game. They had the ball on their 36, third down and a foot to go for a first down. A plunge by one of the running backs would be the conventional call by a conventional quarterback. Lamonica, like Bart Starr or Johnny Unitas, was not conventional. He faked a handoff to a running back, sucking in the defense. Then he lobbed a pass to Billy Cannon all alone behind the Charger defense. Cannon galloped some 50 yards for a touchdown and the Raiders won the game. Later, they won the AFL championship.

Daryle had not played for a winner in college at Notre Dame. During a slack period in Irish football fortunes, Daryle's teams never won more than half their games. "I hated to lose," he told a friend a few days before the Super Bowl. "It was the school of hard knocks for me. But it made me a better competitor. We kept our chins up and never got complacent. Even though we never had a great season, there's a winning spirit at Notre Dame. Just to hear the fight song gets the blood running fast in my veins. It grows on you. It gets bigger and bigger every year. It's in my blood and will be there until I die."

He looked around the practice field as the other Raiders were sprinting through plays. "We've got the same spirit here. This is a young team and the Packers are older and have more experience. They'll be cooler under pressure, maybe, but we have guys who can handle pressure and not let it unravel them."

Over the years Bart Starr had proved he could face the most nerve-shredding situation without unraveling. Yet, oddly, Bart heard many criticisms of his play. "He lacks the daring of a Unitas or a Y.A. Tittle," said the critics. "He follows Vince Lombardi's orders to the letter and never does any thinking himself. He is not a good long passer. That's why he has such a high completion rate. Most of his passes go no longer than 12 yards so they are easier to complete. And he wouldn't even be that good a passer except that the defenses have to concentrate on the good Packer runners."

In his calm, philosophical way, Starr accepted the criticisms. "I really can't say anything about those comments," he said, "because they're true. We have a great defense which gets us the ball, and I'll be the first to admit that a strong running game helps your passing. Our ball-control offense, which concentrates on rushing and short passes, is also a help to me. My arm isn't extremely strong. I couldn't throw

Green Bay's great quarterback Bart Starr takes the ball from center. ➡

the bomb all day the way some quarterbacks do. But the medium-range passing is just right. I wouldn't have been able to become the player that I am on another team."

Starr, typically, was being modest. His passing accuracy, the best in NFL history, could not be explained away simply by saying Starr threw only short passes. In fact, he did throw long passes when a man was open. His passing records were due to Bart's remarkable timing with his receivers. Even as a receiver was cutting to widen the space between himself and a defender, Starr would be winging the ball toward the receiver. When the receiver turned toward Bart, there was the ball, right on top of him. The defender seldom had a chance to bat the ball away.

"I don't let those remarks bother me," Starr said. "I don't care what people say about me, what my image is as a quarterback. I don't believe in taking unnecessary risks, but as long as we're winning, I couldn't care less who people think the best quarterback is."

Bart was sitting in his motel room at Fort Lauderdale. He was wearing a loose yellow shirt and tight green slacks. He looked more like a golfer than a pro quarterback. He was talking about the man who had shaped him into a great quarterback: Coach Vince Lombardi.

"Vince is fantastic for pep talks," he said. "Sometimes he says things in the middle of the week that move me so much, I wish we could play the game right then.

"I don't mean to imply that the speeches are corny. Lombardi is not a corny man. But he says things that need to be said. And I've never heard him say something that wasn't appropriate.

"His pep talks should be recorded. They'd make a big hit with football people. No matter what you might think, football is still an emotional game. Vince knows the pulse of his players. And he knows how to get to their emotions."

Starr rushed off to a team meeting. Last year the Packers, watching game films of the Chiefs, had laughed at some of the Kansas City mistakes. But watching the Raiders, they laughed very little. "They're a better team than the Chiefs," tackle Bob Skoronski whispered to Jerry Kramer. "Right," Kramer said, "they look tough."

One Oakland player who impressed the Packers was Jim (Double O) Otto, the Raiders' center. Jim had played in the very first Raider game, back in 1960, and he had played in every Raider game since, not missing one. Altogether he had played in 122 consecutive games, an AFL record.

Sitting on a trainer's table in the Raider dressing room, Jim talked about the early days of the AFL. He rubbed his large chin thoughtfully. "I was young then and didn't know much," he said with a slight grin. "But I kept telling everybody that the NFL and AFL would play someday even back in 1960.

And I thought I'd be in it because every year I think we're going to win the championship. I'm usually not too excitable watching a football game, but the Super Bowl really gets to me. I watched the Super Bowl game last year in the Coliseum and I kept wanting to run down on the field and help the Chiefs along."

A visitor asked Jim if he felt badly about getting so little recognition as a center. "Nobody ever sees you," the visitor said, "you're buried under a lot of bodies on every play."

"No," Jim said, "I think you're wrong. The fans watch more line play now. Television brings it closer to them. Just make a boo-boo and the fans will let you know. You hear them holler so you know they're watching you."

The fans had no trouble spotting Jim Otto on the field. He wore the numerals "00." "The equipment manager suggested I wear the double-0 because of my last name when I joined the club," Jim said. "I thought it was a good idea. It gave our fans something to smile about, I guess, when we were going so bad in our early days."

Jim grimaced, remembering those painful losing seasons. "Now we've put it all together," he said. "We don't have any superstars like the Packers do. We're all peas from the same pod. Not one famous superstar. But that helps us feel closer and more of a team."

The Packer bus rolled toward the Orange Bowl.

The players were quiet, obviously tense. Each man now knew that Vince Lombardi would not be back as coach. This would be his last game. He would take over as a full-time general manager next season and give the coaching job to his assistant, Phil Bengtson.

The players wanted to give the old man one final victory, one last hurrah. But suppose the Packers lost? Jerry Kramer bit his lower lip at the thought. He had rarely felt so nervous before a football game. He had been so nervous this morning he had put on his shorts backwards.

In the Packer dressing room the players quickly taped their ankles and wrists and put on their uniforms. Today the Packers were wearing white jerseys with green numerals. Jerry Kramer decided he would click on his tape recorder and record, for his book, *Instant Replay,* what Lombardi said in his pregame speech.

"It's very difficult for me to say anything. Anything I could say would be repetitious. This is our twenty-third game this year. I don't know of anything else I could tell this team. Boys, I can only say this to you: boys, you're a good football team. You are a proud football team. You are the world champions. You are the champions of the National Football League for the third time in a row, for the first time in the history of the National Football League. That's a great thing to be proud of.

"But let me just say this: All the glory, everything that you've had, everything that you've won is going to be small in comparison to winning this one. This is a great thing for you. You're the only team maybe in the history of the National Football League to ever have this opportunity to win the Super Bowl twice. Boys, I tell you, I'd be so proud of that I just fill up with myself. I just get bigger and bigger and bigger.

"It's not going to come easy. This is a club that's gonna hit you. They're gonna try to hit you and you got to take it out of them. You got to be forty tigers out there. That's all. Just hit. Just run. Just block and just tackle. If you do that, there's no question what the answer's going to be in this ball game. Keep your poise. Keep your poise. You've faced them all. There's nothing they can show you out there that you haven't faced a number of times. Right?"

"Right!" yelled the Packers.

"Let's go. Let's go get 'em." And the Packers rushed out of the dressing room onto the field at the Orange Bowl.

High up in the stands George Wilson, the coach of the AFL Miami Dolphins, was talking to newspaperman Red Smith. "One big thing in this game," Wilson said, "is that the Packers have been in so many pressure games that the experience has to be an advantage. The AFL has been getting closer and closer to the NFL in talent, but still this has got to be a pressure game for our league. The Raiders have to feel it. I just hope they don't go in too tight."

Daryle Lamonica walked slowly onto the green-carpeted field, feeling the sun warm on his face. A brisk wind was blowing in from one goal toward the other. There were only fifteen minutes until the kickoff. He had never been as tense before a game. Green Bay, he realized, was a magic name in football. Suddenly it hit him in the middle of his chest: this is the biggest game of my life. He couldn't help it; he was very nervous.

Lamonica and his coach, Johnny Rauch, conferred at the sideline, going over the game plan. They planned to run wide sweeps. They hoped to open up the Packer defense and leave it vulnerable to passes.

The Packer defense huddled. "Remember," a coach said, "they like to use sweeps. We have got to cut down those running backs, Dixon and Banaszak, before they can turn the ends and start downfield."

"Let's go," yelled someone else. The Packer defense clapped hands and broke up into twosomes. One player smacked into the other, then the other player smacked into him. They were getting ready for the battle they soon would be fighting at the line of scrimmage—the place the pros call "the pit."

The black-shirted Raiders, their silver numerals gleaming in the warm Miami sun, stood waiting for the kickoff. The white-shirted Packer kicker, Don Chandler, rushed forward and kicked the ball. Oakland's Larry Todd settled under it at the 5. A wave of blockers formed in front of him and he sprinted

past the 10, the 15. Near the 20 the Packers' Tommy Crutcher spun him to the ground.

The Raider offense and the Packer defense trotted onto the field. In the Raider huddle Lamonica called for a sweep to the left by Hewritt Dixon. As Dixon sprinted to the left, he saw a wall of white shirts looming in front of him. He swerved over guard, but there was Packer linebacker Ray Nitschke waiting to slam him down for no gain.

Unable to pierce the Packer defense, the Raiders punted. The Packer offense took the ball on their 34. On the first play Donny Anderson burst through the line for five yards. Then Ben Wilson, a sub who was a surprise starter because Lombardi had a hunch he'd do well, picked up four yards. Next, Starr handed off to Anderson, who sliced off left tackle for four yards and the first down.

"They're not as big as some of the NFL defenses we have faced," Bob Skoronski said to guard Gale Gillingham. "Physically I'm sure we can handle 'em, we can move 'em." The Raider linemen were spaced out in an unusual defense, but the Packer offensive line was having no difficulty knocking them aside, opening holes for the runners. And as Bart Starr often said, "That's where games are won and lost—up front."

The Packers marched across the yard-stripes, reaching the Raider 32. But there the Packer line

Packer linebacker Ray Nitschke (66) sends Raider ball-carrier Hewritt Dixon flying.

missed a couple of blocks, the Raiders throwing Packer backs for losses. On fourth down Lombardi sent in kicker Don Chandler. He stood at the 39, waited as Starr placed down the ball, then kicked the ball through the posts. The Packers led, 3-0.

The Raiders returned the kickoff to their 25. Again Lamonica tried sweeps to the left and right sides. But almost every time he did, there was that quick middle linebacker, Ray Nitschke, waiting in the ball carrier's path to knock him down.

"How does that Nitschke get over there so fast to block those sweeps?" a Raider coach growled.

The answer was two-fold. First, Nitschke was shedding the blocks being thrown at him by the Raiders' tight end. Second, Nitschke and the other Packer linebackers were simply too fast for the Raider running backs, Pete Banaszak and Hewritt Dixon.

The Raiders had to punt, Mike Eischeid kicking the ball out of bounds deep in Green Bay territory— at the 3-yard line. Undaunted, Starr marched his troops steadily upfield against the smaller Raiders. The Packers went all the way from their 3 to the Oakland 13 with short but steady bites of yardage. But there someone again missed a block and Starr was thrown for an 11-yard loss. In came Chandler to kick another field goal. The Packers led 6-0.

Jerry Kramer came off the field dismayed. "Small, stupid mistakes," he muttered to another player, remembering those missed blocks that had cost the Packers two touchdowns. "We should be ahead 14-0 instead of 6-0," a Packer said unhappily.

Out on the field the Raiders were again trying to sweep the ends—still without success. Banaszak twice rolled to the right and in two tries picked up only one yard. The Raiders punted and now Green Bay had the ball on its 38, first down and 10 to go.

And Bart the Cool One was about to strike. One of the Raider defensive backs, Rodger Bird, figured that Bart would call a running play on first down. But Starr was passing. On the snap he saw Bird edging close to the line to cover a running play. Dowler will be one-on-one against his man, Starr thought. Bart looked to Boyd Dowler's side.

Kent McCloughan, the Raider back, bumped Dowler at the line, trying to knock him off-balance. But the bigger Dowler bulled by McCloughan and suddenly he was out "in daylight," as Lombardi would say, all alone. For with Rodger Bird out of position, there was no one else to pick up Dowler. He was running alone at the 50. Starr looped a pass to Dowler. He caught it in full stride at the 40 and raced all the way into the end zone. The Packers had their touchdown. They led 13-0.

The Raiders did not fold. Lamonica decided to give up those sweeps. He sent Dixon and Banaszak plunging straight ahead through quick-opening holes. When the Packer defense bunched up to stop the plunges, Lamonica began pitching short passes to the sideline. The Raiders moved 55 yards to the Green Bay 23. From there Lamonica stepped back to pass. He saw end Bill Miller cutting toward the right corner of the end zone, with linebacker Dave Robinson a few steps behind him. Lamonica arched the pass over Robinson, who leaped for the ball and missed. The ball dropped into Miller's arms and he was in the end zone for the touchdown. The Raiders were back in the game, 13-7.

"I should have dropped back further," Robinson said angrily when he got back to the bench. "I miscalculated and just missed it." No one said anything, all the Packers knowing how badly Robinson felt.

Now came one of the two breaks that would decide this game. With only a minute left in the first half the Packers punted. The Raiders' unlucky Rodger Bird circled under the ball, caught it—and dropped it. The Packers' young Dick Capp flopped on the ball on the Oakland 45. With only a few seconds remaining in the half, Don Chandler kicked the ball from 43 yards out into a stiff wind. The ball soared over the goal posts and the Packers went off the field at the half, leading 16-7.

In the Packer dressing room, Bob Skoronski, Forrest Gregg, Henry Jordan and Jerry Kramer—"the old heads," as Kramer called them—got together in a corner. "Let's play this last 30 minutes for the old man," somebody said. "We don't want to let him down in his last game."

In the Raider dressing room Lamonica and coach Johnny Rauch decided to stick with their pre-game strategy: throw short passes to the sidelines to keep the Packers scattered. But instead of running sweeps, they decided to plow straight ahead. "That Nitschke is just too fast," Daryle said.

All week long Rauch had been telling his defense: "Watch out for a long pass by Starr on a third-down-and-one situation. He likes to fake a plunge, sucking in the defense, then throwing to the open receiver. It's the same play Daryle used against San Diego." The young Raiders had listened and nodded. But now, in the tension of a game, they had forgotten. It would be a lapse they would regret, the second decisive play of this game.

It came early in the third period. The ball was on the Green Bay 40, third and one to go. Lombardi sent in the aging Max McGee, playing his last game as a Packer. "I've set a record this week for going to bed early," McGee told another player before the game. "I hope Vince uses me today."

Starr promptly called for a play he and McGee had often used—the play the Raiders had been warned to watch for. McGee was surprised that Starr had called the play but happy that he had. Here, perhaps, was Max's last chance to contribute to a Packer victory.

Bart took the snap from the center and faked handing the ball to a plunging Ben Wilson. As Bart stepped back with the ball he saw Rodger Bird rush toward the line.

McGee sped past the onrushing Bird. Bart, watching McGee, saw another back coming over to cover him. Calmly, like someone waving to a passing friend, Bart tossed the ball to the other side of Max —away from the approaching back.

Max reacted quickly, turning completely around and catching the ball on his other side. He raced for

the goal line on those aging legs, but the years and that turn-around had slowed him down. He sprinted 35 yards to the Oakland 25, where Bird caught up with him and knocked him down.

Max ran to the bench, his last mission accomplished. "That play," he said later, laughing, "has kept me ten years in this league."

Starr now went to work to finish off the Raiders, who were thunderstruck after being fooled by a play they had been warned to watch for. Bart pitched two passes to Carroll Dale and Donny Anderson that brought the Packers to the 2. From there Anderson cruised through right tackle for the touchdown. Green Bay led 23-7.

The Raiders never stopped struggling, throwing stinging blocks at the Packers, who respected them for their gameness. But the Raiders had no chance. Chandler kicked his fourth field goal, Herb Adderley picked off a Lamonica pass and sped 60 yards for another touchdown, and Green Bay led 33-7. Still feisty, Lamonica slung one long pass to Banaszak, then lobbed a 23-yarder to Bill Miller in the end zone for the Raiders'—and Miller's—second touchdown. A few minutes later the game ended, the Packers the winners, 33-14. Forrest Gregg and Jerry Kramer carried a grinning Lombardi off the field on their shoulders, his hail and farewell as a Packer coach.

Veteran Max McGee, playing in his last game for the Packers, is tackled from behind after setting up a Green Bay touchdown.

"The Packers took away our sweep," a disconsolate Jim Otto was saying in the Raider dressing room. "When we started running up the middle, we began to gain ground. But we were behind by then and had to throw to catch up. Maybe it would have been different if we ran up the middle from the start."

Old Double-0 looked at the floor, his pants grimy with grass stains, his face smeared with sweat-caked dirt. "We didn't get any breaks," he said. "And when they got a break, they did something with it."

In the crowded Packer dressing room Al Silverman of *Sport* magazine gave another set of car keys to Starr. He had been named the game's Most Valuable Player for the second year.

"He deserved it," said Oakland tackle Tom Keating. "The big difference between that team and other teams is Bart Starr. He is unbelievable. He comes up to the line and starts looking around. And you can see it: he knows what defense we're in. It's as if he had been listening in on our defensive huddles. He sort of smiles, he looks like he's laughing at you. But he knows, he knows."

The bruised Packers praised the grit of the Raiders. "They never gave up," Henry Jordan said. "Oakland is as good as some NFL teams. In next year's Super Bowl the game will go right down to the wire."

Victorious Vince Lombardi is carried off the field by his players after Green Bay's 33–14 victory.

SUPER BOWL II
(Played in Orange Bowl, Miami, Fla., January 14, 1968)

Scoring by quarters:

	1	2	3	4	Totals
Green Bay Packers	3	13	10	7	33
Oakland Raiders	0	7	0	7	14

Scoring plays:

Team	Period	Elapsed Time	Scoring Plays	Packers	Raiders
Packers	1	5:07	Chandler, field goal (39)	3	0
Packers	2	3:08	Chandler, field goal (20)	6	0
Packers	2	4:10	Dowler, 62-yd. pass from Starr	12	0
			Chandler, conversion (kick)	13	0
Raiders	2	8:45	Miller, 23-yd. pass from Lamonica	13	6
			Blanda, conversion (kick)	13	7
Packers	2	14:59	Chandler, field goal	16	7
Packers	3	9:06	Anderson, 2-yd. run	22	7
			Chandler, conversion (kick)	23	7
Packers	3	14:59	Chandler, field goal (31)	26	7
Packers	4	3:57	Adderley, 60-yd. interception return	32	7
			Chandler, conversion (kick)	33	7
Raiders	4	5:47	Miller, 23-yd. pass from Lamonica	33	13
			Blanda, conversion (kick)	33	14

Team Statistics

	Green Bay	Oakland
Score	33	14
Touchdowns	3	2
P.A.T.	3	2
Kick (A-M)	3-3	2-2
Field Goals (A-M)	4-4	1-0
First Downs	19	16
Rushing	11	5
Passing	7	10
Penalty	1	1
Total Offense	322	293
Rushing	160	107
Passing	162	186
Passing		
Attempts	24	34
Completions	13	15
Had Intercepted	0	1
Yards Gained	162	186
Touchdowns	1	2
Punting		
Number	6	6
Yards	234	264
Average	39.0	44.0
Punt Returns		
Number	5	3
Yards	35	12
Average	7.0	4.0
Kickoff Returns		
Number	3	7
Yards	49	127
Average	16.3	18.1
Penalties		
Number	1	4
Yards	12	31

SUPER BOWL III

New York Jet quarterback Joe Namath.

Joe Said It Would Be So

JOE NAMATH STRODE toward the microphone. Several hundred people, seated at tables, applauded. It was a warm Thursday evening in Miami three days before Super Bowl III. The Miami Touchdown Club was presenting Joe Namath with an award for his accomplishments during the 1968 AFL season. He had been the leader of a New York Jet team that had won the AFL championship. On Sunday the Jets would face the NFL champions, the Baltimore Colts, in the Super Bowl.

In his drawling way Joe spoke to the audience about the season. He told how the Jets had come from behind to win games that seemed hopelessly lost. He said he knew the NFL Colts were 18-point favorites to beat the Jets in the Super Bowl.

"Most people don't give us a chance," Joe said. "I think we have a chance."

He paused, smiling. "Matter of fact," he said very slowly and clearly, "I think we'll win it. I'll guarantee it."

The listeners applauded, admiring Joe's courage. But the next day people smiled when they read what Joe Namath had said. "The Jets are probably the worst AFL team to play in the Super Bowl," said one football fan. "And the Colts look to me every bit as good as the Packers were a year ago. How can you expect the Jets to come even close to the Colts?"

The Colts seemed almost invincible. Their great passer, Johnny Unitas, had been bothered by an aching right elbow all season long. However, his replacement was a tested veteran named Earl Morrall. Morrall had led the NFL in passing during the season. The Colts had won 13 of 14 games, becoming only the third team in the history of the NFL to win that many games. They had conquered the big, tough Minnesota Vikings to win the Western Conference championship and swept over the Cleveland Browns, 34-0, to win the NFL championship. In the Cleveland game the Colt defense had swarmed all over the Browns' offense, blitzing through the line to bury the Brown quarterback.

The Jets had not been nearly as impressive. They had won 11 of 14 games to win the AFL's Eastern Division title. One of their losses had been to last-place Buffalo. Then they had squeaked by the Oakland Raiders, 27-23, to win the AFL championship.

"Joe Namath is unquestionably a great passer," said one expert a week before the Super Bowl. "And he has two great pass catchers in Don Maynard and George Sauer. But the Baltimore blitz will smash through the New York line and overwhelm Namath.

And the Baltimore line, with big men like Bubba Smith, will pile up the New York runners."

The cocky Joe Namath was sure the Jets could pass and run against that Baltimore defense. When the Jets had arrived in Florida, Joe sported a flowing Fu-Manchu-style mustache and long hair and wore a mod double-breasted suit. He proclaimed loudly to a friend in the Fort Lauderdale airport, "We should be favored by nine or ten points."

One afternoon soon afterward he met Lou Michaels, the Colt place-kicker, in a restaurant. He and Lou were old friends.

"Joe," said Lou, "we're going to kill you."

Joe laughed. "You don't have a chance, man," he said.

"We'll beat you by thirty points," Lou said, a thin edge of anger in his voice.

"You've really got to be crazy," Joe replied. "You're not even going to win the game. . . ."

As Joe talked, Lou became angrier. He said that Johnny Unitas could come off the bench and beat the Jets. Joe disagreed. He may have been great in his prime, Joe said. "But now, he can't throw across the street." It seemed for a moment that the two would come to blows. But then Joe laughed and they both calmed down.

When the Jet players read that Joe was saying the Jets would win, some of them worried. They were afraid that he would get the Colts all fired up.

Joe had good reason for his cockiness. First of all,

he knew what he could do on a football field. Against a fierce pass rush, no one could release a ball faster than Joe Willie Namath. He had proved himself as an All-America at the University of Alabama and as Jet quarterback for the past four years. He had helped to lift the Jets from near-bottom in the AFL to the championship.

Secondly, he had noticed some interesting things in films of the famous Baltimore pass-blitz. He had seen Rick Volk and Jerry Logan, the two safeties, move up to the line and crash through holes in the defense to knock down the quarterback.

"No matter who blitzed, they had to leave part of the middle open," Joe wrote in his autobiography, *I Can't Wait Until Tomorrow*. "I knew I could hit my wide receivers slanting in . . . I just prayed that the Colts would blitz us. If they did, I figured, they were dead."

The Jets' coaches also thought that the team's two runners, Emerson Boozer and Matt Snell, could run against the Colt defense. The Jets' stumpy coach, Weeb Ewbank, had noticed the aggressive play of the Colts' left linebacker, Mike Curtis. He decided that the Jets would run at the other side of the Colt line against end Ordell Braase and linebacker Don Shinnick.

It was a good decision for reasons that even Ewbank didn't know. The Colts tried to hide the injury, but Braase had injured his back. On Sunday he would be in pain and would not be the rock on defense that he usually was.

Several Colt players were watching films of Namath throwing against Oakland in the AFL championship game. "He sure throws a lot of passes," an assistant coach said.

"At least fifty of them in this game," a player said.

"And a lot of them are those long ones down the sidelines to Don Maynard."

"They should be kind of easy to intercept—especially since we know he likes to pass so often. We can be ready for the long pass."

"We have to get a real strong pass-rush on Namath, though," said the coach. "If you give him time to look for those open receivers, he will murder us."

Bubba Smith, the massive 295-pound Colt guard, was matched up against Dave Herman. It was a good matchup for the Colts. Herman weighed only 255 pounds, 40 pounds lighter than Bubba. Shula and the Colt coaches were hoping to see Bubba bowl over Herman and knock down Namath on the pass rush.

The coaches and quarterbacks Johnny Unitas and Earl Morrall were impressed by the Jet linebackers—Ralph Baker, Al Atkinson and Larry Grantham. They decided to key on Atkinson, the middle linebacker. If he moved to the left, the Colts would throw to the right, and if he moved to the right, they would throw to the left.

Coach Shula also decided to use a lot of draw plays. By faking a pass and handing off to one of the running backs, he hoped to keep those Jet lineback-

ers frozen in place for a moment, looking for the run. This would slow down their rush on pass plays.

Both Unitas and Morrall, after looking at the movies, thought they could pass to the areas covered by Jet cornerbacks Randy Beverly and Johnny Sample. "Both of them will give our receivers a lot of room," Morrall said. "We should be able to toss short passes into their areas."

Joe Namath was sprawled on his back by the side of the swimming pool at his motel in Fort Lauderdale. He was wearing short trunks and sunglasses. Several newspapermen sat down near him. One of them asked Joe, "How can you be serious when you say the AFL team should be the favorite in the Super Bowl?"

"Heck," Joe said, "there are five or six quarterbacks in the AFL—myself, Johnny Hadl, Daryle Lamonica, Bob Griese—who are better quarterbacks than Earl Morrall. That's just a plain statement of fact."

The writers were startled. At previous Super Bowls only Fred (The Hammer) Williamson had been brash enough to say he thought the AFL had better players than the NFL. "We've got another Hammer here," one writer whispered to another.

Joe went right on talking. "How many NFL

Earl Morrall, who led the Colts to the NFL championship, gets set to pass against the Jets.

teams have a quarterback who could complete many passes to their wide receivers?" he asked the reporters. "Those are the tough ones to complete, not those passes that you dump off to your backs. In our league we throw much more to our wide receivers than they do in the NFL. I completed 49 percent of my passes this season but I could have completed 80 percent if I had dropped the ball off to my backs the way they do in their league. You put any quarterback in the NFL on our team and only a few wouldn't be third-string."

No NFL quarterback would be first-string on the Jets, Joe was saying. No NFL quarterback would take his job away from him.

"You have got to believe Joe when he says the Jets are going to win. He has a way of doing what he says he is going to do."

The speaker was Fred Klages, a Chicago White Sox pitcher who had played against Joe when both were growing up in western Pennsylvania. Fred had come to Miami to see the Super Bowl game. "You name it," Klages said, "baseball, football, basketball. There was nothing Joe Namath couldn't do and do better than anybody else."

Klages told about a big basketball game between his school and Namath's Beaver Falls High School team. A conference championship was at stake. "It was the last minute," Klages said. "We are ahead by a point and they have the ball. There's ten seconds to go and they give the ball to Namath. He's about

30 feet out and he starts to bounce it nice and easy. The fans begin to count, nine, eight, seven—and he keeps right on bouncing.

"When the countdown gets to two, Joe lets go. He pops a one-hander from 30 feet out. Then, while the ball is still in the air, he turns around to face the fans, his back to the basket. He raises his two hands in the air, with two fingers of each hand sticking up to form a V. The ball is still in the air and he is telling the crowd the ball is going to go through the net for two points to win the game.

"And, sure enough, the ball goes through the hoop—and they beat us for the title. How was that for self-confidence? After that, whatever Joe Namath says, I believe him."

Walt and Lou Michaels were brothers. But Walt and Lou were not speaking to each other. Lou Michaels, who had argued with Joe Namath, was the place-kicker and part-time lineman for the Colts. Walt Michaels was an assistant coach for the Jets. They were not speaking to each other because they had agreed: "One of us might say something about our team that might help the other. It's better we don't speak until after the game."

But they had talked on the telephone a few weeks before the Super Bowl.

"Let's make a deal," one brother said. "Whoever gets the $15,000 winner's share will give $7,500 of it to Mom."

"Good idea," the other brother said.

No matter which team won, Mrs. Michaels would win, too.

It was Sunday, Super Bowl time again in Miami. It was partly cloudy and the temperature was in the 70s. Clouds scudded across the sky, blown by a soft northerly wind. The Jets' bus rolled south on the superhighway toward Miami. Seated alone, Joe Namath stared out at the flat countryside. In his mind he suddenly saw Don Maynard racing down the sideline and free for a pass. He could see himself leaning back and arching a long pass that dropped into Maynard's arms.

Suddenly the scene dissolved and he saw a new one. He saw a Colt safety blitzing. He saw tight end Pete Lammons dash into the area left open by the blitzing safety. He saw himself throw a dart-like pass to the open receiver. Beautiful, he thought, beautiful.

Near the front of the bus sat Johnny Sample, a veteran who was one of the leaders of the Jet defense. Once he had played for the Colts—in 1958 and 1959 when they won the NFL championship. Then he had been traded away by the Colts and released by his new team after he had argued with one of the coaches. Today Sample was going to show the NFL that he was good enough.

Weeb Ewbank, the Jet coach, remembered those championship games with the Colts in 1958 and 1959. He had been the Colt coach. After 1959 the Colts had slumped and Weeb had been fired. Today

Weeb had a good reason for wanting to defeat the Colts. He, too, had something to prove—his ability as a coach.

The Baltimore Colts quietly slipped on their uniforms in the Orange Bowl dressing room. A veteran team, many of them older than 30, they had come together for a dozen big games over the past ten years. They had played in NFL championship games in 1958, 1959, 1964 and 1968. They were no strangers to tension. They knew how to use tension to sharpen their concentration.

Earl Morrall rubbed a hand across his black crew-cut. One of the players walked over to him. "Today you'll get your chance to show that pop-off Namath how good a quarterback you are, Earl." Morrall smiled. He had been playing in the NFL for a dozen years. He wasn't overly concerned what young quarterbacks said about him.

He glanced at a play-book. Shula had suggested a play that might work against the Jets. It was the old flea-flicker play, the kind sometimes tried in a backyard game of touch football. Earl thought it might surprise the Jets and succeed. On the play he handed off to Tom Matte, who ran toward the sideline, then stopped, turned and flipped the ball back to Earl. If they were fooled, the Jet defense would be heading for Matte and Morrall would have time to look downfield and find an open receiver.

The Colts kicked off to the Jets, who ran the ball

Namath barks out the count to
the Jets in Super Bowl III.

back to their 23. Immediately Joe Namath tested out the right side of the Baltimore line, to see if the Jets could run against it.

"Nineteen straight on three," Namath said in the huddle. On the count of three he took the snap and handed off to Matt Snell. The 220-pound fullback ran straight behind the Jet left tackle, massive Winston Hill. The 6-foot-4, 275-pound Hill smashed into Ordell Braase, the Colt right end who was pained by a sore back. Braase grunted at the impact, reeling backward. Hill drove Braase to the right. Snell cut to the left and gained three yards before he was tripped up.

"Nineteen straight on two," Namath said in the huddle, calling the same play. Hill bumped Braase even more to the right. Snell ran to the left for nine yards to the Jet 35. The young Colt safety, Rick Volk, slammed into Snell and knocked him down. Snell jumped up, but the dazed Volk was stretched out on the grass. He was carried off the field.

The Jets now knew they could run against the Colts' right side. Joe probed for other weaknesses. With the ball on the Jet 31, second down and 14 to go, Namath knew the Colts would be expecting him to pass. "I hope they blitz, I hope they blitz," he said to himself as he walked up to the line.

On the snap Joe saw a linebacker blitzing toward him. He looked for Matt Snell to slant into the open space where the linebacker had been. And there was Snell. Namath flipped a short pass over the middle. The big fullback grabbed the ball and dashed nine yards downfield before cornerman Bobby Boyd cut him down from the side.

Now Joe Namath knew he could pass against the feared Baltimore blitz. And he could run against the vaunted Baltimore line. But the Baltimore defense stiffened and forced the Jets to punt.

The Colts took the ball on their 27. The big Colt line, led by the veteran Bill Curry at center, was eager to smash into the younger players on the Jet line. Play after play they drove back the Jets. Then Morrall passed to tight end John Mackey, who ran right over Jet safetyman Jim Hudson to gain 19 yards. The Colts seemed to be gaining at will, almost swaggering as they marched to the Jet 19. But then receiver Willie Richardson dropped a pass, Morrall overthrew a receiver, and then was nabbed after trying to run.

On fourth down Lou Michaels came in to try for a field goal. The ball was placed down on the 27. The pudgy Michaels kicked, as his brother Walt on the Jet bench rooted for him to miss. And Michaels did miss, the ball curving away from the goal posts.

Namath trotted onto the field with his offense. He had been a little surprised at how easily the Colts had moved the ball against the Jet defense. "Maybe they're going to score a touchdown or two," he thought. "It just means we've got to score a few more."

On the bus he had seen Maynard in a day-dream flying down the sideline. Now, in the game, he really sent Maynard down the sideline—what the pros call a "fly pattern." He saw Maynard burst ahead of the Colt safetyman. He threw a long pass but it dropped a foot beyond Maynard's reaching hands.

Maynard admitted in the huddle that he was having trouble with his leg. "You should have told me," Joe said, "and I would have taken a couple of inches off the pass."

The Jets had to punt. Now Morrall had the ball. He looked at the two Jet cornerbacks, the veteran Johnny Sample and the young, thin-faced Randy Beverly. Morrall was sure his two tricky receivers, Willie Richardson and Jimmy Orr, could get open against Beverly and Sample. On third down on his 45, Morrall went back to pass, looking for Willie Richardson, who was making one of his quick moves against Sample. But Johnny Sample was "up" for this game and he stuck with Richardson. Morrall threw to Richardson, but Sample stuck out a hand and knocked away the ball.

Near the end of the first period the Colts got the first break of the game. George Sauer caught a pass from Namath at the Jet 15, and was hit by the Colts' Lennie Lyles. The ball popped out of Sauer's arm and was recovered by a Colt. Baltimore had the ball on the Jet doorstep—at the Jets' 12-yard line.

The Colts punched to the Jet 6. On third down Morrall stepped back to throw. He saw tight end Tom Mitchell sprinting across the rear of the end zone all alone. Morrall threw a whizzing pass, but a Jet ticked it with his hand at the line. The ball flew toward Mitchell but slightly behind him. Mitchell twisted, trying to grab it, but the ball hit his shoulder pad and caromed away—right into the hands of a diving Randy Beverly. The Jets had intercepted in the end zone. Now *they* had gotten a break.

The ball was placed on the 20. Suddenly the Jet offense came alive. Guard Bob Talamini and tackle Winston Hill began punching holes in the Colts' right side. Whenever the Colt defense sent a blitz rampaging toward Namath, Joe stung the Colts with a pass to an open receiver.

Snell ran three times for a first down. Then he swept the right side for 12. Namath saw a blitzer coming and threw a line drive to halfback Bill Mathis for a gain of six to the Jet 46. He threw to George Sauer for 14, then again to Sauer for 11. The Jets stood at the Baltimore 34. The crowd roared.

So far the Colts' big tackle, the 295-pound Bubba Smith, had not placed a hand on Namath. The gritty Dave Herman, some 40 pounds lighter, had knocked down Bubba time after time. Herman was making quick, lightning-like moves to the left or right, then chopping down the huge Bubba from the sides. "I got to be quicker," Bubba kept saying to himself, but he could not evade Herman's chopping blocks.

In the huddle Joe decided he wanted to look at the Colt defense before he called the next play. "I'll call the play on the line," he told the Jets. "Be ready to go on one," meaning the ball would be snapped on the first count. Then, standing over the center

and scanning the defense, Namath decided on a play. In code he called out the play to the Jets, who had to listen intently to hear it above the crowd's roar. But they heard it, and at Joe's first "hut" they smashed into the Colts, driving for another Jet first down.

A few minutes later, on the Colt 9, Joe stood over the center and shouted at the Jets, "Nineteen-straight." Again he handed off to Snell. Again Bob Talamini and Winston Hill drove Braase and Shinnick to the right, Snell cutting to the left and gaining five yards to the 4. "That Snell is great," Hill said. "Some of those runners want a hole big enough

Fullback Matt Snell steps into
the end zone, scoring the Jets'
only touchdown.

to back a truck through. But Matt just wants a little
room and he'll slice his way through."

With the ball on the Colt 4, Joe saw a familiar
face coming into the game for the Colts. It was his
old debating partner, Lou Michaels. Namath rea-
soned that with Michaels in there, the Colts would
use a five-one "goal line" defense. And he knew the
play that would work beautifully against that defense.

He crouched down in the huddle. "Nineteen-
straight," he said. "And we'll go on the first sound."

Even if Namath only cleared his throat, the ball
would be snapped. The Jets assumed their three-

point stance. "Now," Joe yelled. The ball was snapped. Hill and Talamini slammed into the right side of the Colt line. They drove back Braase and Shinnick, who had been caught unprepared for the suddenness of the onslaught. Namath handed the ball to Snell, who spun through the opening and into the end zone.

At 5:57 of the second period the Jets led 6-0. For the first time in a Super Bowl game, an AFL team led an NFL team. Jim Turner kicked the extra point and the score was 7-0.

The Colts took the ball on the kickoff and again they were on the move. They marched quickly to the Jet 38. But on a third-down pass play, Johnny Sample, sticking surprisingly close to the receivers, tipped a pass away from receiver John Mackey. Lou Michaels came in for another field-goal try and again he missed.

The Jets stormed back again, piercing the right side of the Colt line repeatedly. Snell picked up three or four yards on almost every carry. But then, going back to pass on third down, Joe Namath was dumped. Jim Turner attempted to kick a field goal from the 41 but the ball dropped short.

Now it was the Colts' turn to rampage down the field against the lighter Jets. On one play Tom Matte burst through the Jet line and dashed 58 yards to the New York 26. He was caught from behind by safety Billy Baird.

The Colts forged to the Jet 17. Morrall went back to pass and tossed to Willie Richardson at the goal line. Again, there was Sample, hanging close. He leaped high for the ball and plucked it away from Richardson. Another Jet interception had stymied the Colts and stolen away a touchdown.

The Jets had to punt once again. With 30 seconds remaining in the half, the Colts had the ball on the Jet 42. In the huddle Earl Morrall called for that razzle-dazzle flea-flicker play. He handed off to Matte, who ran wide toward the left sideline. Suddenly Matte stopped, whirled, and lateralled the ball back to Morrall.

The shocked Jets turned to run back toward Morrall. In the confusion, receiver Jimmy Orr had sneaked off alone. He was standing in a corner near the goal line jumping up and down, waving his arms so that Earl Morrall would see him.

But Earl didn't see Orr, his view obstructed by the swirl of white-shirted Jets rushing toward him. He hastily threw downfield to Jerry Hill, but Jim Hudson of the Jets veered in front of Hill and intercepted the ball.

The dejected Colts walked off the field for the half-time intermission, losing 7-0 to a team they were supposed to wallop by some 20 points. In the clubhouse coach Don Shula told his sore-armed passing ace, Johnny Unitas, to be ready to play in the second half. Johnny nodded. The Colts seemed a little uncertain. Nothing that they had tried so far against the Jets had succeeded in getting them points.

Right at the start of the second half, another

Big Bubba Smith, the Colts' defensive star, slaps
Namath's arm as he lets go of the ball.

break went against the Colts. Tom Matte fumbled and the Jets recovered on the Colt 34. With Snell running to the right side and Joe Namath flipping short passes over the middle, the Jets marched steadily to the Colt 11. But Bubba Smith, for the first and only time in the game, shot through and knocked Namath for a long loss. The Jets lined up to try for a field goal, and Jim Turner kicked the ball through the uprights from the 32. The Jets led 10-0.

Now the Colts seemed to be pushing the panic button. Morrall missed Mackey on a pass. He threw to Jerry Hill—but for no gain. On third down he ran out of the pocket and a Jet slammed him to the ground. As the punting team went out onto the field, a worried, frowning Don Shula told Johnny Unitas to get ready to go into the game.

The Jets' offense had the ball on their 32. Namath continued to call many plays at the line of scrimmage rather than in the huddle and he succeeded in moving the ball to the Baltimore 32. Then a finger in Joe's throwing hand went numb and he had to leave the game for a minute until the feeling was restored and he could pass again. Babe Parilli, the second-string Jet quarterback, came in to replace Joe. He missed a pass on third down and the Jets decided to try for a field goal. Parilli placed the ball down at the 32 and Jim Turner booted it in a high arc over the crossbar. The Jets led 13-0.

A huge roar erupted when the crowd saw the old master, Johnny Unitas, trot onto the field with the Colt offense. The Jets glanced at each other. Unitas was a wizard at penetrating defenses. How would they do against him?

The Jets held off Unitas until well into the fourth period, meanwhile building up their lead. They led 16-0, Turner having kicked another field goal, this one from the 9-yard line. It was his third of the day.

Then, suddenly, Johnny U. began to look like his old self. He masterfully mixed passing and running plays, hitting open receivers at the sidelines. The Colts moved deep into the Jets' territory. From the Jet 25, Unitas stepped back and saw Jimmy Orr running in the end zone. He tossed a near-perfect pass that spiraled straight toward Orr's hands. But Randy Beverly, playing with the persistence that had won him a job in a tryout camp, turned on the speed to jump high in front of Orr and intercept, saving another touchdown.

But Unitas would not be stopped. When the Colts got the ball again, he led them 80 yards for a touchdown. Jerry Hill plowed over the stacked-up Jet defense from the 1. The Jets now led 16-7.

The Colts used an on-side kick on the kickoff. It traveled only 15 yards, and the strategy worked: a Colt fell on the free ball. Now the Colts seemed to have the momentum that carries teams to victory.

Again Johnny U. dazzled the Jets. He dropped the ball into a receiver's hands in the left flat, then on the right sideline, then over the middle. The Jets'

Pass defender Randy Beverly gets set to run after intercepting a Baltimore pass intended for Jimmy Orr (28).

defenders were always just a step or two away from the receivers. The Colts arrived at the Jet 25. But three plays gained only six yards and now it was fourth down and four yards to go from the 19.

There were about two and a half minutes to play. If the Colts kicked a field goal, they would be behind 16-10, within one touchdown of beating the Jets. There still might be time enough for Johnny U. to pass the Colts from one end of the field to the other. He had done it often enough in his career. He was a wizard at scoring last-gasp touchdowns. But coach Shula decided against the field goal and went for the first down. Unitas stepped back and threw to Orr. He missed and the Colts lost the ball on downs.

Now the result of this third Super Bowl was almost certain. The Jets were ahead 16-7 with less than two minutes to play and they had the ball. As the final seconds ticked off on the big Orange Bowl clock, a smiling Namath paced the sideline, shaking the hands of his teammates. "You told us so, Joe," one said.

"I guaranteed it," Joe said happily.

When the gun sounded, the referee picked up the ball and handed it to Larry Grantham, a linebacker with the Jets since the early 60s, when they had been called the Titans. "Thank you," Larry said and with pride he walked off the field, ball tucked under his arm.

The Jets swept into their dressing room, laughing and cheering. "Out, out, all you NFL writers," Namath was yelling at the press. "Where are all the ones who said we would lose by 18 points? I hope all you writers eat your pencils and pads." He laughed.

Someone asked him if he felt sorry for Earl Morrall. "Better him than me," Joe said. Then, recalling his prediction that the Jets would win, he said, "How do you think people would have been on us and on me if we had lost?"

Someone asked if he regretted what he had said during the week. "No, I meant every word of it. I never thought there was any question about our moving against their defense. I'm sorry that Don Shula thought what I said about Morrall was a rap. I only meant it as a statement of fact."

Joe saw a slender man wearing a straw hat moving through the crowd of reporters. Joe pushed his way toward the man and hugged him. The man was crying, the tears running down his cheeks. "Oh God, you did it, boy," said Joe Namath's dad. "You did it."

In the Colt clubhouse the players wandered around the room dazedly, as though they were hypnotized. Big Bubba Smith, who had been beaten so badly by Dave Herman, stared at the floor. "It's going to be tough to go back home after this," he said in a low voice. "I'm going to start working right away for next year."

Looking grim, Shula talked to reporters. "I don't think we did anything right," he said. "Our defense didn't play well and our offense couldn't come up with the big plays. They broke down our right side on defense and once they found that successful, they stuck with it."

Don Shinnick, who had been driven back so often by Winston Hill and Bob Talamini, said he felt sick about his play. "I thought I was as ready as I've ever been," he said. "But you can't tell about those things. I guessed wrong a few times and I missed a couple of tackles that I should have made. Then, when I did make a good play, it seemed like somebody else would guess wrong or miss a tackle. Maybe it was poor concentration, maybe we weren't quite as ready as we thought we were."

"You gave up the ball five times—on four interceptions and one fumble," a writer said sympathetically. "They gave up the ball only once—on a fumble."

"There's the game right there," Shinnick said.

In the Jet dressing room Bob Talamini, who had punched out those holes in the right side of the Colt defense, was talking to a friend about the importance of this victory to every AFL player. "My career has more meaning now," Talamini said, a smile on his face. "I can hold up my head with anyone. Like a Gene Hickerson at Cleveland or a Jerry Kramer with Green Bay. Like them, I've been part of a world championship team. We don't have to apologize to anyone. We're it."

That night the Colts' Rick Volk, who had been

Jet lineman Bob Talamini gives his son Bobby a victory kiss after the game.

hurt when he collided with Snell early in the game, was rushed to a hospital. He had collapsed at the team's hotel. Doctors discovered he had suffered a brain concussion. He was told to rest in the hospital for a few days.

The next afternoon flowers arrived at the hospital for Volk. With the flowers was a card wishing Volk a quick and full recovery. The flowers and the card were from Joe Namath.

SUPER BOWL III
(Played in Orange Bowl, Miami, Fla.,
January 12, 1969)

Scoring by quarters:

	1	2	3	4	Totals
New York Jets	0	7	6	3	16
Baltimore Colts	0	0	0	7	7

Scoring plays:

Team	Period	Elapsed Time	Scoring Plays	Jets	Colts
Jets	2	5:57	Snell, 4-yd. run	6	0
			Turner, conversion		
			(kick)	7	0
Jets	3	4:52	Turner, field goal (32)	10	0
Jets	3	11:02	Turner, field goal (30)	13	0
Jets	4	1:34	Turner, field goal (9)	16	0
Colts	4	11:41	Hill, 1-yd. run	16	6
			Michaels, conversion		
			(kick)	16	7

Team Statistics

	New York	Baltimore
Total First Downs...............	21	18
First Downs Rushing............	10	7
First Downs Passing............	10	9
First Downs by Penalty..........	1	2
Rushes.........................	43	23
Yards Gained Rushing (net).....	142	143
Average Yards per Rush.........	3.3	6.2

	New York	Baltimore
Passes Attempted	29	41
Passes Completed	17	17
Had Intercepted	0	4
Tackled Attempting to Pass	2	0
Yards Lost Attempting to Pass	11	0
Yards Gained Passing (net)	195	181
Total Net Yardage	337	324
Punts	4	3
Average Distance Punts	38.8	44.3
Punt Returns	1	4
Punt Return Yardage	0	34
Kickoff Returns	1	4
Kickoff Return Yardage	25	105
Yards Interception Returned	9	0
Fumbles	1	1
Opponents' Fumbles Recovered	1	1
Total Return Yardage	34	139
Penalties	5	3
Yards Penalized	28	23
Total Points Scored	16	7
Touchdowns	1	1
Touchdowns Running	1	1
Touchdowns Passing	0	0
Extra Points	1	1
Field Goals Attempted	5	2
Field Goals Made	3	0
Total Offensive Plays	74	64
Avg. Gain per Offensive Play	4.6	5.1

SUPER
BOWL IV

"President Nixon Is on the Phone"

THE DAPPER COACH, Hank Stram, stood up in the steamy dressing room. He stared at the 40 players seated on stools or sprawled on the concrete floor. The Kansas City Chiefs were dressed in faded pants and torn jerseys, ready to go onto the practice field. Now Stram was telling them what kind of a team they would be facing in Super Bowl IV.

"The Minnesota Vikings are a very basic team," he said. "They line up and dare you to beat them. They remind me a lot of the Green Bay Packers."

He had to say no more to inspire the Chiefs to win this Super Bowl game. The memory of their humiliating loss to the Packers in the first Super Bowl lingered in the mind of each Chief. "I have never been able to look at the films of that game," defensive end Jerry Mays once said. "Maybe one day I will— when we win a Super Bowl game."

Kansas City quarterback Len Dawson.

107

Most fans had been surprised to see the Kansas City Chiefs representing the AFL in this Super Bowl game. During the 1969 season the Chiefs had finished second to the Oakland Raiders in the AFL's Western Division. But as part of the AFL playoff system that season, the second-place teams in both conferences got a second chance at the league championship and the Super Bowl. First they played the first-place team in the other conference. If they won, the first-place team was eliminated and a second-place team played in the AFL title game.

First the Chiefs had flown to New York to take on Joe Namath and his Jets, who had won the Eastern Division title. On a cold day at Shea Stadium they had squeaked by the Jets, 13-6. On that same weekend the first-place team in the West, the Oakland Raiders, demolished the East's second-place team, the Houston Oilers, 56-7. Thus the Raiders would meet the Chiefs for the chance to go to the Super Bowl.

The Raiders had seemed almost certain to beat the Chiefs. But the underdog Chiefs surprised the Raiders, beating them 17-7. The Chiefs were on their way to the Super Bowl. But many AFL fans thought the league was being represented by its second-best or third-best team. "The Raiders and the Jets are better than the Chiefs," many said.

The AFL fans were especially disappointed to see the Chiefs go to the Super Bowl because this would be the last game between the AFL and NFL. Next season all teams would be in the enlarged NFL.

"This is the last chance for the AFL to get even in the Super Bowl," said an AFL fan. "We've won one and lost two. If the Raiders or the Jets were playing in the Super Bowl this last time, we'd have a chance to make it two won and two lost. But the Chiefs—they don't stand a chance of beating the Vikings."

Certainly there was no doubt about who was the best team in the NFL. It was the Vikings, who played in the NFL's tough Central Division—what the players called "the black and blue division." In that division the Vikings had won 12 of 14 games. In the playoffs they had subdued the Los Angeles Rams and their famous defensive line 23-20 and rolled over the Cleveland Browns 27-7. Now, to win the world championship in the Super Bowl, all they had to do was to beat this second-place AFL team.

This game would mean more than a championship. Coaches and fans would be evaluating two different styles of football. The Vikings played strong, bruising, straight-ahead power football, like the Packers before them. Few tricks. The Chiefs, on the other hand, were full of tricks. On defense they hopped around like fleas, confusing opposing linemen, who sometimes couldn't decide which man to block. On offense quarterback Lenny Dawson rolled out behind a moving wall of blockers to pass, instead

A determined Kansas City defense faces the powerful Vikings.

of dropping straight back and standing in a pocket. "With a moving pocket to the left or right," Coach Stram explained, "a blitzer can't be sure where he will find the passer." And Stram had signed a group of small "mini" running backs, like 5-foot-9 Mike Garrett, to scoot through quick-opening holes in the line. When the defense bunched up in the middle, those quick backs could race like mice to the outside.

"This will be the new football," Hank Stram said the week before the Super Bowl. "The trend of the '60s was basic simplicity in pro football as shown by the Packers and the Vikings. The trend of the '70s will go to a more varied type of game. Most teams advertise what they are going to do by lining up in the same formation. I believe in using a lot of different formations to create doubt. Variety in all phases of the game will be the trend of the '70s. You might say that this game is a meeting between the old and the new."

Most people thought that the old would win. The Vikings were favored by two touchdowns.

"DAWSON LINKED TO GAMBLERS."

The headlines were large and black. They ran across newspaper front pages from coast to coast the week before the Super Bowl. A TV sportscaster had reported that Kansas City Chief quarterback Len Dawson was under suspicion of knowing members of a nationwide syndicate of gamblers. Dawson said he had done nothing wrong. NFL Commissioner Pete Rozelle publicly defended the Chief quarterback.

"We have no evidence that Len Dawson is guilty of having anything to do with gamblers," Rozelle declared. But suddenly Len Dawson was shouldering the weightiest burden of his life. While he prepared and studied for a Super Bowl game, he had to worry over the shameful publicity. He was concerned that people would taunt his young son and his wife, saying that he was a crook.

He said nothing to his teammates about the burden he carried. Not much of a talker anyway, he was even more close-mouthed than usual. It had been a painful year for him. His father had died. Then, limping on aching knees weakened by repeated injuries, he was told he would need an operation. He refused the operation because he didn't want to miss the season—but often the knees hurt. And now this.

He never complained. He worked hard at practice, then usually went off by himself. But his eyes gave him away: they showed pain and worry. His teammates understood why.

"Lenny Dawson is innocent, but that won't matter to a lot of people when we play against the Vikings," one Chief was telling a visitor one day. "Let Lenny throw an interception, let him fumble a handoff at a bad time, and you can be sure everyone will be saying that Lenny threw the game. He has to go out there and do his best not to make any mistakes for two reasons. So we can win and so no one can say he is a crook. That's an awful lot of pressure to put on one man."

"They say we are underdogs," the Chiefs' raw-boned wide receiver, Otis Taylor, said several days before the Super Bowl game. "We think we have a great team. And we're much more mature than the team that played Green Bay. We talked big before that one, at least some of the guys did."

Otis didn't say so, but he seemed to be referring to Fred (The Hammer) Williamson, who was no longer with the team. "I think those guys talked big," Otis said, "because it was a way to hide their . . . well, their apprehension. I don't want to say fear.

"We have great new people, unselfish people. This is the game we've all been waiting for, the pot of gold, ever since we lost that first one to Green Bay."

Huge Buck Buchanan, the 6-foot-7, 290-pound defensive tackle, overheard what Taylor had said. "I'll tell you something," Buck said. "After that Green Bay game I pounded on a chair in the dressing room and said over and over, 'I want them again, I want them tomorrow.' "

Buck smiled. "Well, the Packers aren't here. But it's the same thing, the Packers or the Vikings, they're both NFL." And then, slowly, Buck said, "And now it's tomorrow."

Len Dawson, unhappy about it, was getting most of the publicity while the Viking quarterback, Joe Kapp, was getting little during the week before the Super Bowl. Yet Joe Kapp was the more colorful of the two. A tough-talking guy who liked fast cars and all the luxury things in life, Joe had come out of the University of California to play pro football in Canada. There he won a championship and picked up the nickname Injun Joe. He looked like a battle-scarred Indian. His chin was crisscrossed with the scars of dozens of battles, on and off the football field.

He came to the Vikings from Canada in 1967. He gave the team a relaxed, happy attitude that it had lacked. Once he and middle linebacker Lonnie Warwick were arguing.

"I'm right," Warwick yelled.

"I'm right," Kapp snarled.

"Let's go outside and settle this."

They went outside the hotel room. Warwick looped a right-hand punch that dropped Joe Kapp to the floor. Injun Joe got up slowly, rubbing his bruised chin. "You're the toughest man I've ever met," he said to Warwick. "Let me buy you dinner." And Joe threw an arm over the startled Warwick's shoulder and took him out to dinner, the fight forgotten.

Hank Stram was worried about his pass defense. Johnny Robinson, the Chiefs' veteran safetyman, was recovering from a rib injury. Stram knew that the Vikings' speedy wide receiver, Gene Washington, could go deep "for six," as the players say, at any time. He was counting on Johnny Robinson to cover Washington. But now there was a question

whether Johnny could play.

"I think I can play," Robinson said. "I hope so. I really want to play so bad I can taste it."

Johnny Robinson had been playing in the AFL since the league began in 1960. He had played in the first AFL games, now he would be playing in the last game by an AFL team—in the Super Bowl. If his ribs stopped hurting.

Viking coach Bud Grant had worked out his game plan. He was particularly concerned about having a big play. His best big play was the long pass to Gene Washington. If Washington was double-teamed, John Beasley would be open for passes over the middle.

Hank Stram was talking to the Chiefs' offensive unit. Most important, he told them, they had to protect Dawson on pass plays. They decided to double-team the two Viking ends, putting two blockers on each of them. As for Dawson, he was to take advantage of the Viking pass defense by throwing short passes in front of the defenders.

Johnny Robinson and Len Dawson were rooming together. On the Saturday night before the Super Bowl, Dawson was seated on a bed flipping through the Chiefs' play book. The time was almost eleven

The Vikings' scrappy quarterback Joe Kapp gets set to pass from his own end zone.

o'clock. Robinson was in too much pain to sleep and Dawson was too nervous.

A little later they turned out the lights and tried to sleep. Dawson turned and tossed fitfully, thinking how important this game was—to his team, for himself. He had to play well tomorrow, he had to.

Sometime in the night, Dawson woke up with stomach cramps. He switched on the light and looked at the time. It was four o'clock in the morning. Robinson was awake too. Neither of them was able to sleep, so for the next few hours Johnny and Len read the newspaper sports pages about the game tomorrow. "They don't give us a chance," Johnny said.

The Chiefs' bus rolled into the Sugar Bowl parking lot in New Orleans, site of the fourth Super Bowl. The players filed down a long tunnel to their dressing room. Inside, draped over hangers in each stall, were their red jerseys. On the left shoulder of each jersey was a red-white-and-blue patch with the words "10 AFL." The AFL Commissioner had given special permission to wear the patch for the game. It was a way of saluting the ten-year history of the AFL.

The players stared at the emblems. This was the league once ridiculed in the newspapers and by the NFL. Today, in the AFL's final game, the Chiefs would have the last chance to prove that the AFL was now the equal of the older league.

"Let's not disgrace this AFL patch out there

today," someone said.

Len Dawson nodded. He was pale and he looked tired after getting so little sleep. He looked over at Johnny Robinson and saw him wince as he pulled off his shirt.

The phone rang in the Chiefs' dressing room. "A call for you, coach," an assistant said to Hank Stram. "President Nixon is on the phone."

Astounded, Stram picked up the phone. The President said he had decided to call because he admired the way Len Dawson and the Chiefs were trying to come back from adversity. He said he hoped the young people of the country would see the Chiefs play well today, watching on TV as he was doing, and admire their ability to come back. He wished Stram, Dawson and the Chiefs good luck.

Stram thanked the President. After hanging up, he told the players that the President of the United States was watching them and wishing them good luck. A little later the Chiefs went out to meet the Vikings.

Out on the field the Purple People Eaters were warming up. They were the Vikings' towering defensive line: the 6-foot-6, 265-pound Carl (Moose) Eller; the 6-foot-5, 250-pound Gary Larsen; the 6-foot-4, 260-pound Alan Page; and the 6-foot-4, 260-pound Jim Marshall, whose hobby was sky-diving. As big as they were, they could run as fast as most halfbacks. They had been called the Purple People

Eaters because the Viking color is purple and because they seemed to eat up opposing ball carriers.
The two ends, Carl Eller and Jim Marshall, had
crashed through blockers to knock down passers so
often during the season that Hank Stram was now
assigning two Chiefs to each one of them.

Carl Eller pointed to a banner in the stands. It
read: "Go, Purple People Eaters." Eller, who was an
actor during the off-season, smiled and said to Marshall, "I sure hope we go."

Under a leaden sky, the air a cool 61 degrees inside the Sugar Bowl, the red-jerseyed wave of Chiefs
dashed forward for the kickoff. Jan Stenerud, a Nor-
wegian-born kicker who hadn't even understood the
game of football when he was a college senior, ap-
proached the ball at an angle, soccer-style, and
kicked it through the end zone.

From the 20 the Vikings slogged straight ahead.
On second and seven from his 35, Kapp stepped
back to pass. He saw two Chiefs trailing Washington
as he dashed downfield. As the Vikings had sus-
pected, tight-end John Beasley was free as he cut
across the middle. Kapp slanted a pass to Beasley,
who caught the ball at the 50 and stampeded to the
Chiefs' 39. The crowd cheered, surprised by the suddenness of the Viking attack. But two plays failed
and a third-down pass to Beasley ticked his fingertips and fell incomplete.

It was fourth down and 10 to go from the Kansas
City 39. A field goal attempt seemed certain. But

Viking coach Bud Grant could feel the strong 15-mile-an-hour wind blowing into the Vikings' faces. The wind, he thought, would blow back a kick from that distance. Fred Cox, the Viking kicker, did not have a long range. Grant decided on a punt that he hoped would pin the Chiefs inside their 10, where they might fumble, lose the ball and create an easy Viking touchdown.

The Vikings' Bob Lee punted, aiming to kick the ball out of bounds at the 5. But he kicked too cautiously, and the ball bounced out of bounds at the 17.

In the grandstand and in homes across the country, the second-guessers were loud in their scorn. The Vikings should have tried for the three points, they said. If the Vikings lost this game by three points, Bud Grant would hear about that punt for the rest of his life.

A few minutes later the Chiefs' Jan Stenerud, kicking with the wind at his back, tried for a field goal from the 48—and made it. In the second period Stenerud kicked another field goal for the Chiefs—this time from the 32-yard line, this time *into* the same wind that had been blowing against the Vikings. The Chiefs led 6-0.

Halfway through the second period the Chiefs took the ball on the Minnesota 44. Len Dawson, although still woozy after his near-sleepless night, noticed that the Viking defense was bunching up in the middle. He decided to send one of his fast "mini" runners shooting to the outside.

In the huddle Len stared at his team with those clear blue eyes and said, "Fifty-two reverse go. On two." It was an end-around play.

At the line he scanned the defense. The Viking ends, badgered all afternoon as two men hit them at the same time, were creeping away from their tormentors—toward the middle of the line. "Hut . . . Hut . . ." Len was shouting.

He took the snap and wheeled around. He saw end Frank Pitts coming toward him. He handed off to Pitts who kept on running toward the opposite sideline. At the sideline he swerved around a blocked Viking linebacker and sped downfield.

Pitts raced to the 25 before being dragged down. But there the Purple People Eaters rose up and threw back three Chief plays. Jan Stenerud trotted into the game and kicked a 25-yard field goal into the wind, his third straight. Now the Chiefs led 9-0.

A few seconds later came the first of three plays that would decide the outcome of this game. On the kickoff the Vikings' Charlie West camped under the ball, caught it, and then dropped it. The Chiefs fell on the ball at the Viking 19-yard line.

Dawson sent his tiny "mini-backs" scooting up the middle, past the frustrated Purple People Eaters, who were being knocked aside by those two-man blocks. Then Dawson lobbed a short pass to Otis Taylor in front of the cautious Viking secondary, for

Soccer-style kicker Jan Stenerud looks like a dancer after kicking one of Kansas City's three field goals.

10 yards. Now he was on the Viking 5-yard line, third down and five to go for a touchdown.

At the sideline coach Hank Stram was hoping he didn't have to settle for a fourth field goal. He thought it would hurt the Chiefs' morale, having failed to score a touchdown in four consecutive invasions of Viking territory. At the other sideline Viking coach Bud Grant hoped the Purple People Eaters could stop this third-down play. Stopping this try for a touchdown would lift his team's spirits.

Dawson looked over the Viking defense. Then he saw a substitute trotting in from the Chief bench. Stram was sending in a play. The sub whispered in Len's ear. "Five toss power trap."

Len nodded: a good play. It was a run up the middle by the Chiefs' fastest back, 5-foot-9 Mike Garrett. Len thought the play might work since the Vikings, remembering that end-around sweep, were spreading out and opening up the middle.

Viking tackle Alan Page edged a few inches to the outside, expecting another Chief run to the sideline. On the snap he saw Chief tackle Jim Tyrer pull out from the line and start to run toward the sideline. Then he saw Len Dawson start to pitch the ball out to a halfback running toward the sideline.

An end run, Page thought. He broke for the sideline. As he did he was flattened by a block by Chief guard Mo Moorman, who caught Page as he turned. At the same moment tight end Fred Arbanas had knocked middle linebacker Lonnie Warwick toward the other sideline with a body-shuddering block.

And Len Dawson, instead of pitching out to a half-back, was handing off to little Mike Garrett.

Mike threaded his way through the middle of the Viking line and saw a four-foot wide channel. Alan Page was knocked to one side, Lonnie Warwick to the other. Garrett sped untouched through the channel and into the end zone. That second decisive play had given the Chiefs a touchdown. Stenerud kicked the extra point, and the Chiefs led 16-0.

At the halftime intermission the Vikings told each other, "Sixteen points won't beat us. We've been a great second-half team all season long."

And they seemed on their way to proving it as the third period began. Moving swiftly like the thundering Vikings of the 1969 season, they covered 69 yards in 10 plays. Dave Osborn muscled over left tackle for the touchdown. The score was Chiefs 16, Vikings 7, midway through the third period. A worried young linebacker for the Chiefs, Jim Lynch, said to an assistant coach, "They're a good second-half team. I hope we can hold them."

Now came the third decisive play that would take the worry off the Chiefs' minds. After the kickoff the Chiefs rolled from their 18 to the Viking 46, going part of the distance on another end sweep by Pitts.

Dawson called for a pass to the tall, swift Otis Taylor. On the snap Taylor ran toward the sideline, in front of the Viking backs. Dawson pitched a short pass that Taylor grabbed at the Viking 41.

Up rushed the Vikings' Earsell Mackbee and dived at Taylor's legs. But as Mackbee slammed

into Taylor, Mackbee's left arm, which had been injured earlier in the game, suddenly went numb.

Mackbee couldn't hold on. The quick Otis stepped out of Mackbee's grasp and fled down the sideline. Coming at him on a collision course was safetyman Karl Kassulke.

The tricky Taylor swerved toward midfield. Kassulke tried to reverse direction and Taylor, catching him off-balance, pushed him away with a solid straight-arm. Then Taylor whirled away and dashed for the end zone. He crossed it with a gleeful smile on his face, hurling the ball high into the air. The Chiefs led 23-7, and now the Vikings had to play frantic catch-up football.

Joe Kapp tried to roll out of the pocket, but the Chiefs' stacked defense contained him. Kapp tried to zip a short pass to John Beasley slanting over the middle. But Johnny Robinson, wincing with the pain of those sore ribs, soared high to intercept it. Linebacker Willie Lanier intercepted another, cornerback Emmitt Thomas a third. A little later the gun went off and the Vikings trudged off the Sugar Bowl turf the disappointed losers, 23-7.

In the losers' dressing room Viking coach Bud Grant said the Chiefs had outplayed his team today. But he couldn't help looking back on that touch-

Surrounded by Viking tacklers, Mike Garrett crosses the 5-yard line. He fought them off and scored the Chiefs' first touchdown.

down pass to Otis Taylor that had put the game out of reach. "We had two shots at him," he said. "If we had stopped that pass, we might have come back the way we were building up momentum. . . ."

Len Dawson sat on a stool in the Chief dressing room, his face pale, sweat beading on his forehead. He held a paper cup filled with a soft drink, and his right hand trembled as he brought the cup to his lips. All the emotions of the week were draining out of Dawson and that trembling right hand showed how strong those emotions were.

Reporters asked him if the gambling stories had put pressure on him. "Sure I felt it," he said in his soft-voice. "I couldn't concentrate. I'd try to drive it out of my mind by getting out my play book at night, studying it and our game plan. I played this game a lot of times this week." He laughed. "The older I get the more nervous I get."

A voice cut through the din of the dressing room. "Lenny, the President of the United States is on the phone. He wants to speak to you."

"The President wants to talk to me?"

"Yes."

Len got up and walked to the phone. President Nixon congratulated Len on his victory. Len said thank you. "But I didn't do it myself," he told Mr. Nixon. "Everybody did a great job."

The President said that from what the FBI had told him, there was no truth to the stories connecting Len with the gamblers. And the President added

Len Dawson talks to President Nixon after the game.

that by coming back from adversity, he would be an inspiration to young people.

"Mr. President," Len said, "I certainly appreciate that and I hope that we can, because we try to exemplify what is good in professional football."

A little later Len was standing in the middle of the Chief dressing room. He pointed toward his roommate, Johnny Robinson. "I don't know how he played," Len said to a friend. "He was in such pain last night. But he played a great game."

At that moment Joe Foss strode into the room. A lean World War II fighter-pilot ace, he had been the AFL's first commissioner from 1960 to 1966. He walked over to Johnny Robinson. The two men, who had been with the AFL since its first games, hugged each other. They had seen the AFL begin; and now they had seen it end—in victory.

SUPER BOWL IV
(Played in Sugar Bowl, New Orleans, La., January 11, 1970)

Scoring by quarters:

	1	2	3	4	Totals
Minnesota Vikings	0	0	7	0	7
Kansas City Chiefs	3	13	7	0	23

Scoring plays:

Team	Period	Elapsed Time	Scoring Plays	Vikings	Chiefs
Chiefs	1	8:08	Stenerud, field goal (48)	0	3
Chiefs	2	1:40	Stenerud, field goal (32)	0	6
Chiefs	2	7:08	Stenerud, field goal (25)	0	9
Chiefs	2	9:26	Garrett, 5-yd. run	0	15
			Stenerud, conversion (kick)	0	16
Vikings	3	10:28	Osborn, 4-yd. run	6	16
			Cox, conversion (kick)	7	16
Chiefs	3	13:38	Taylor, 46-yd. pass from Dawson	7	22
			Stenerud, conversion (kick)	7	23

Team Statistics

	Minnesota	Kansas City
Total First Downs	13	18
First Downs Rushing	2	8
First Downs Passing	10	7
First Downs by Penalty	1	3

	Minnesota	Kansas City
Rushes.......................	19	42
Yards Gained Rushing (net).....	67	151
Average Yards per Rush.........	3.5	3.6
Passes Attempted.................	28	17
Passes Completed...............	17	12
Had Intercepted...............	3	1
Times Tackled Attempting Pass...	3	3
Yards Lost Attempting Pass......	27	20
Yards Gained Passing (net)......	172	122
Total Net Yardage................	239	273
Punts............................	3	4
Average Distance Punts.........	37.0	48.5
Punt Returns....................	2	1
Punt Return Yardage...........	18	0
Kickoff Returns..................	4	2
Kickoff Return Yardage.........	79	36
Yards Interceptions Returned......	0	24
Fumbles.........................	3	0
Opponents' Fumbles Recovered...	0	2
Total Return Yardage............	97	79
Penalties.......................	6	4
Yards Penalized.................	67	47
Total Points Scored..............	7	23
Touchdowns...................	1	2
Touchdowns Running..........	1	1
Touchdowns Passing............	0	1
Extra Points..................	1	2
Field Goals Attempted..........	1	3
Field Goals Made..............	0	3
Total Offensive Plays............	50	62
Avg. Gain per Offensive Play....	4.8	4.4

SUPER
BOWL V

Baltimore rookie Jim O'Brien, who was called "Lassie" by his teammates because of his long hair.

Lassie Had a Dream

THE TWO ROOMMATES were quietly hanging up their clothes. They had just arrived at their motel near Miami. There was a knock at the door. Johnny Unitas strode to the door, opened it and asked the visitor, a newspaperman, to come in. Only a few days before a game as big as Super Bowl V, Johnny Unitas was his usual cool and affable self. "This is no bigger game than any other," he said with his crooked grin. "The only thing is, there is a lot more money to be won."

Johnny's roommate flopped down on a couch to answer the visitor's questions. The roommate was Earl Morrall, who had gone away from Super Bowl III slump-shouldered and dejected. He had been criticized for not seeing Jimmy Orr all alone in the end zone and failing to throw him the pass that could have won that Super Bowl for the Colts.

"It was one of the biggest games of my career," Earl was saying. "And it didn't turn out too well. I've tried to shrug it off, but I just can't. I keep

135

thinking about it, and I still get flashbacks, remembering all the bad things.

"I still don't know why I didn't look for Orr. There's no way I can explain it, even to myself. What made it such a bad mistake was that Orr had been the primary receiver. And yet when I saw Jerry Hill cutting across the middle, I threw to him." He looked sadly at the floor. "I think back on it often," he said.

At Super Bowl V it didn't seem likely he would get the chance to make a similar mistake. Johnny Unitas again was the starting quarterback, and Earl Morrall was the substitute. Unitas had won back his job by leading the Colts to a conference championship during the 1970 season.

This year the Colts had been in the new American Football Conference, which was made up of the 10 former American Football League teams and three old National Football League teams—the Colts, Steelers and Browns. In this Super Bowl, representing the AFC, they would face the Dallas Cowboys, the best team in the National Football Conference, which was made up of 13 former National Football League teams. Thus Super Bowl V was a contest between two former NFL rivals.

The Colts came to the Super Bowl with wise old heads like Johnny Unitas, and some strong young bodies, notably the 220-pound Norm Bulaich. A rookie, Norm had been the Colts' top running back in 1970. Another rookie who had helped was field-goal kicker Jim O'Brien. The Colts had won 11 of 14

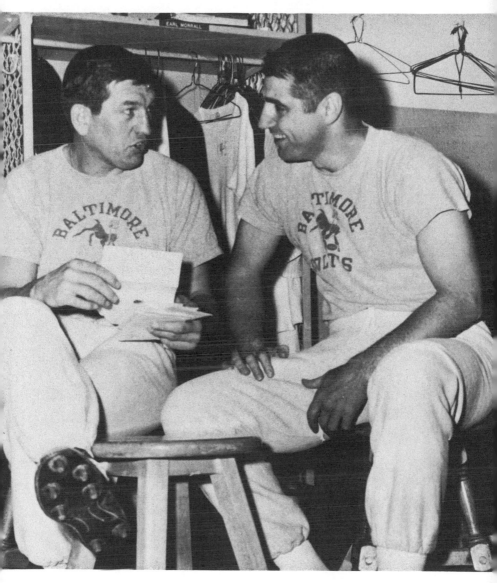

Baltimore quarterbacks Johnny Unitas and Earl
Morrall chat before the game.

games, the second-best record in pro football in 1970.

A typical game for the Colts was their battle with the Oakland Raiders for the American Football Conference championship. They led 10-0 on a short plunge by Bulaich and a field goal by O'Brien. But then 43-year-old George Blanda of the Raiders kicked a 48-yard field goal and the Raiders closed to within seven, 10-3. Oakland quarterback Daryle Lamonica was hurt a few minutes later and Blanda ran into the game. He pitched the Raiders to a quick touchdown to tie the game 10-10.

Unitas quickly sparked the Colts downfield. O'Brien kicked another field goal. Then Bulaich took a Statue of Liberty handoff from Unitas and scored. The Colts were 27-17 winners. They headed for the Super Bowl with dreams of avenging their humiliating loss to the New York Jets two years earlier in Super Bowl III.

For the Dallas Cowboys the climb to the Super Bowl heights had been much steeper and more slippery. In a big game against their division rivals, the St. Louis Cardinals, the Cowboys lost 38-0, and seemed out of the race with a 5-4 record.

Then at a meeting of defensive veterans, Herb Adderley, the old Packer now with the Cowboys, spoke up. "I never played on a team with a record worse than eight-won and six-lost. I am not going to start now," he said. These four, Adderley, Lee Roy Jordan, George Andrie and Bob Lilly, were the heart of the defense. They resolved that they would never be buried by a high score again. From then on, the defense stood firm against so many onslaughts that someone said, "you couldn't score against them till doomsday." The Dallas defense became known as the Doomsday Defense.

Coach Tom Landry, meanwhile, was having a talk with quarterback Craig Morton. Morton was depressed by the loss to the Cardinals. In that game he had played as though he were handcuffed, throwing weak passes that were intercepted or easily batted down by the Cardinals. He hadn't put a point on the scoreboard. The shrewd Landry, a lanky former defensive back, told Craig that he thought the quarterback was worrying so much about calling the right plays that he wasn't concentrating enough on his passes. Landry told Greg that from now on he would call the plays.

"A quarterback should call all the plays," Craig insisted. "No quarterback likes to give up part of his job."

The stern-faced coach overruled him. "From now on," Landry declared, "I'll call every play by sending a man in from the sideline with a play. You concentrate on just one thing: hitting the open receiver."

The change helped Craig Morton and the Cowboys. Craig hit 60% of his passes during the rest of the season, compared to 40% previously. The Cowboys won five straight games to win in their division. Then they beat Detroit 5-0, and San Francisco 17-

10, for the NFC championship. Now they had the chance to win the NFL championship in the fifth Super Bowl game.

The two teams flew to Florida. The game had been shifted back from New Orleans to Miami's Orange Bowl. As the Colts warmed up under the hot Florida sun, they recalled their last visit to the Orange Bowl. "That Colt team was a great team," tight end John Mackey told a friend one day after practice. "But we just didn't get prepared. We brought down our families and too many of the guys were more concerned about going to the beach than playing ball.

"This year we came alone. Our families will come later, on the day before the game. This time I think we are going to be prepared. I don't think any of us want to go through what it was like after we lost to the Jets. I remember feeling like I wanted to dig a hole and hide in it until the next season started."

The Dallas Cowboys also had come to Miami with something to avenge. For four straight years they had climbed as high as playoff games, coming within one or two games of winning the NFL championship. Each time they had failed to go all the way. "This is the team," someone once said, "that always goes to the loser's bowl."

One of the Cowboy stalwarts on defense was 6-foot-5, 260-pound Bob Lilly, a broad-shouldered, red-haired giant. It was said that he had once picked up a Volkswagen at the curb and deposited it on a sidewalk.

He was strolling toward the football field near Miami, where the Cowboys were practicing. A writer, talking to him, suddenly asked: "Why can't the Cowboys win the big ones? Is it because they choke up under pressure?"

Lilly stared at the man. "Why don't you wait until Sunday night and ask the same question?" he said angrily. "We've heard that question so often. Maybe, after the Super Bowl is over, we'll have a better answer than any answer I could give you now."

Johnny Unitas met a visitor to the Colt camp, a blond man from Green Bay, Wisconsin, named Bart Starr. Starr wished his old rival luck and they talked about the 1970 Colts. The conversation soon turned to Norm Bulaich, the rookie running back, who had improved steadily all season. Johnny didn't say so, but he had helped Norm to be a better runner. Early in the season Norm had fumbled several times. He began to carry the ball with two hands. But by carrying it that way, he lost some of his speed and body balance, and he was easier to pursue and knock down.

One day Johnny took Norm by the elbow in the dressing room. "Look," Johnny said, "stop thinking about fumbling and just run. If I had worried about interceptions, they would have run me out of the league years ago."

Norm began to run so well he led the team in rushing with 426 yards. He gained most of those yards on short plunges, the tough kind, never going for more than 15 yards. Norm got his toughness from his summer jobs while he was a student at Texas Christian University. First he was a roustabout in the Texas oil fields, and later he became a longshoreman, unloading heavy cargoes from ocean-going ships.

"I unloaded barrels of rice," he explained. "It's hot work, 200 degrees is what it feels like, but the pay is $4 an hour, $6 if you work nights. I'll be back in the spring unless something better comes along."

"You'll be getting a big raise from the Colts," he was told, "and you won't have to work as a long-shoreman."

Norm smiled. But later he said, "I'm no hero who is going to make a big salary. I'm still just a rookie who makes too many mistakes. I'm just another guy who carries the ball through holes and for a long time I wasn't doing that well."

By season's end, however, he was doing well. In a playoff game against Cincinnati, he picked up 116 yards in 25 tries. After the game Norm ran with the other Colts to the locker room, peeled off his uniform and pads, and went to the showers. When he came back he saw something sitting in the corner of his stall—a football.

Without saying anything, the other Colts had told him what they thought of his performance: they had given him the game ball.

Rookie Jim O'Brien, the place-kicker, was combing his hair, which was very long. The other Colts were always telling him to get a haircut and calling him Lassie because of his shaggy hair. Jim didn't mind. A 25-year-old bachelor who had left the Air Force Academy because he didn't like being ordered what to do, Jim lived his own life, "doing my own thing," as he said.

Five nights before Super Bowl V, Jim went up to his motel room, watched television for an hour or so, then jumped into bed. In a few minutes he was asleep. He began to dream. He saw the Orange Bowl, the crowd up and roaring, the score tied, late in the game. The two teams were lined up, one team set to kick a field goal that would win the game, the other team trying frantically to block it. Looking down at the field in his dream, Jim tried to see who the kicker was: Mike Clark of Dallas or himself. But he couldn't see the kicker's face and then he woke up. He didn't go to sleep for a while, wondering whether it was he or Mike Clark in that dream. He woke up and rolled over. "It was only a dream," he said to himself, and soon he had fallen asleep again.

They called him The Animal. They said it to him—to his face. Once his teammate, Tom Matte, introduced him to an unsuspecting fan. "This is Mike Curtis," Tom Matte said.

"The Animal," the fan howled, leaping back in fright.

Mike was not amused. "That The Animal stuff got out of hand," Mike was telling Matte and some of the other Colts a few days before the Super Bowl. "True, when I'm on the field I am an animal, I guess. But when I'm off it I'm a gentleman."

Indeed he was wild on a football field, even in practice. A linebacker, he attacked passers with a frenzy. Several times in practice he slammed his 232 pounds into Johnny Unitas, who got up screaming at Mike. At another practice he threw a punch at Colt center Bill Curry, who was his best friend on the team. "He's just wild," said one Colt, summing up the way all the players felt about Mike Curtis. "I'm glad he's on our side."

What still rankled Mike was losing to the Jets two years ago. "Going into the game," he said, "I continually heard you've got to beat that long-hair, that Joe Namath. Yes, I thought, we've got to beat that long-hair. But there was no dishonor in losing to the best—and that's what Namath was. Losing to the other Jets, dirty players like Johnny Sample, that was degrading."

In that game the Jets had run plays away from The Animal—to the opposite side from where he was stationed. But now Mike had shifted from right linebacker to middle linebacker. Unlike the Jets, the Cowboys were going to have to run right into The Animal's lair.

Someone asked Mike which was more important to him—the $15,000 winner's share or the world championship ring given to the Super Bowl winner.

"The money is unimportant," he said grimly. "I want the ring."

"Our defense and our running game got us to where we are, and that's what we are going to rely on in the Super Bowl."

Speaking was gangling Tom Landry, a fedora perched on his balding head. He was outlining to writers how the Cowboys were preparing for the Colts. He talked about the Cowboy running game. He mentioned Duane Thomas, a 220-pound running back who had been so outstanding in 1970 that he had forced Calvin Hill, the 1969 rookie of the year, to the bench.

"Thomas is the guy who started us on our winning streak after we lost to the Cardinals," the tall coach said. "I think the toughest thing in football is to combat a running team. They just keep knocking your linemen back. And then you can't do the things you want to do—like rush the passer. So a good rushing team makes its passing attack more effective."

The Dallas passing attack seemed to need help. Craig Morton had passed well in the last half of the season, but he had passed weakly in the two playoff games that the Cowboys had won. He completed only four of 18 against Detroit, the Cowboy Doomsday Defense winning this "baseball-scoring" game, 5-0. In that game Bob Hayes, the speedy pass-catcher, curled into the Detroit zone defense and was standing alone time after time. Morton threw

passes over Hayes' head and into the grass at his feet, seldom hitting him for a completion. In the playoff game for the championship of the NFC, a 17-10 victory over the 49ers, Morton completed only seven of 22.

One trouble with Morton, people said, was that he wanted his teammates' respect so much. Because he wanted it so badly, he worried that he might fail them. And when you worry about failing, as Johnny Unitas could have told him, you are more likely to fail.

Dallas was depending on its Doomsday Defense to blunt the passing of Unitas and the running of Norm Bulaich. Up front there were titans like 6-foot-6, 260-pound Jethro Pugh and the 6-foot-5, 260-pound Bob Lilly, and the 6-foot-6, 250-pound George Andrie. The three linebackers—Lee Roy Jordan, Dave Edwards and Chuck Howley—were thought to be the best threesome in the NFL. Unitas and Morrall already had been warned by the Colt coaches, "Try not to pass into Howley's area. He is excellent at defending against the pass."

The deep backs could run with the fastest receivers. "Up until last year we always had a weak spot at cornerback," Lee Roy Jordan said. "But then we made that trade with Green Bay and got Herb Adderley. Now, with him and Mel Renfro, we've got

Duane Thomas, the Cowboys' rookie running back, runs past Baltimore's Bubba Smith.

the two best cornerbacks in the business."

Most teams who played San Francisco in 1970 had put two men on receiver Gene Washington. But Renfro covered Washington alone for half a game and once intercepted a pass to the flying Washington that set up a Dallas touchdown in the 17-10 victory.

Bob Hayes had been an Olympic sprinter. In the 1964 Olympics at Tokyo he won gold medals in the 100-meter and 400-meter relay races. "That was my biggest thrill," he was telling Herb Adderley one day at practice. "Not even a victory in the Super Bowl could be the equal to that."

After graduating from college, he decided to try to be a pro football player. He had played football in college but as a fullback. He wasn't big enough to be a pro fullback. He came to the Cowboys to try out as a pass-catcher. He had small hands and the hard passes of pro quarterbacks ripped open the skin between his fingers. Bob Hayes went on "playing with the small hurts," and he learned how to grab the ball despite his small hands. He also learned very quickly that he couldn't count on his speed alone to run away from defenders and be free for a pass. Those defenders were almost as fast as he; they could stay within a couple of feet of him and bat away passes. Bob Hayes learned how to cut and feint to put more air between himself and a defender. Then, when he did catch a pass, there would be a foot-race between himself and a defensive back for the goal-line, and in that kind of race Bob figured to win.

In the 1970 season he had caught 34 passes. Ten of those 34 catches went all the way for touchdowns. He ran 89 yards for one of those touchdowns. No receiver in pro football was more dangerous to a defense than Bob Hayes going deep for the bomb.

It was the Saturday before the Super Bowl. The Colts were finishing their last practice. Jim O'Brien was kicking field goals. No. 2 center Tom Goode was snapping the ball to Earl Morrall, who placed the ball down for Jim.

"Hey, rook," yelled veteran defensive tackle Billy Ray Smith, who would be retiring after tomorrow's game. "You're going to miss this one—you're going to blow it—you'll blow it!"

Jim O'Brien grinned. Billy Ray was always yelling at him like that—what O'Brien called "scream drills." A year earlier the Chicago Bears had screamed at Lou Michaels before a field goal. Michaels missed the field goal. Ever since then the Colts prepared their field-goal kicker for the screams of the other team by having Billy Ray scream at the kicker like a crazed banshee.

The time was a few minutes after two, the big crowd of 80,000 settled into their seats at the Orange Bowl. The temperature was a humid 70, the sky covered with clouds. A whistle shrilled through the damp air, rookie Jim O'Brien rushed forward to kick the ball, and the crowd's roar rose over the stadium. Super Bowl V, which would be the closest and most thrilling so far, had started.

It was, most of all, a game of mistakes. The first mistake was Baltimore's. On the Colts' most dangerous play, Johnny Unitas threw a low pass that Dallas linebacker Chuck Howley dove for and intercepted. Howley skidded along the grass with the ball, then jumped up and ran it to the Baltimore 46. But Dallas' offense, looking clumsy, could not move any deeper and had to punt.

Mistake No. 2 was more costly for Baltimore. The Colts' usually sticky-fingered kick returner, Ron Gardin, dropped a punt and it was recovered by Dallas on the Baltimore 9. But on three tries Craig Morton could not move the Cowboys any closer, his third-down pass sailing over a receiver's head. Mike Clark ran in to kick a field goal. He rammed the ball through the uprights and Dallas led 3-0.

A little later, with the ball on the Dallas 47, Morton settled down and arched a long pass to Bob Hayes, who sped all the way down the sideline to the Baltimore 12. But again the Cowboy offense moved backward instead of forward. The Cowboys had to settle for three points instead of seven. Clark kicked a field goal from the 30 and Dallas led 6-0.

Then came the most bizarre play in Super Bowl history. On third down and 10 from the Baltimore 25, Unitas danced back to pass. He saw wide receiver Eddie Hinton slanting across the middle at the 45. Unitas threw but the ball shot high above Hinton's head. The young receiver leaped for the ball. It struck his finger tips and glanced upward. Running near Hinton was Dallas back Mel Renfro, who reached for the ball. It grazed his fingertips. Behind Renfro there was Colt tight end John Mackcy.

A Unitas pass, already touched by Colt Eddie Hinton and Cowboy Mel Renfro (left), heads for Colt John Mackey (88). He caught the ball and scored.

He saw the ball bounce off Renfro's finger tips and arch toward him. Mackey grabbed the ball. There was no one in front of him. He ran some 50 yards to the end zone. Touchdown for the Baltimore Colts. The score was tied 6-6.

In the press box one writer turned to another and shouted, "That play was illegal. Two pass receivers can't touch the same forward pass."

"Yes, they can," said another. "They can if a pass defender touches the ball after one pass receiver has touched it, as Mel Renfro did. That makes the pass legal."

With the score tied, Jim O'Brien ran onto the field to kick the extra point. The ball was snapped to Earl Morrall, who placed it on the ground. O'Brien stepped forward, swinging his right foot. As his foot came into the ball, it skidded against the ground. O'Brien kicked the ball weakly and a Dallas lineman batted it down. The extra-point try had been blocked, and the score was still tied 6-6. That missed point could decide the game. Jim walked slowly off the field, wishing he could drop into a hole and disappear.

Now came Mistake No. 3. Unitas, trying to run, was tackled by Lee Roy Jordan and fumbled the ball. Dallas recovered on the Baltimore 28. Throwing short passes, Craig Morton moved the ball to the 7. From there he lobbed a pass to Duane Thomas in the end zone. Mike Clark kicked the extra point and Dallas led 13-6.

The next mistake, or turn-over of the ball, cost

Baltimore their valued Johnny Unitas. Going back to pass, Johnny was hit hard by Dallas' George Andrie. Johnny threw, but the weak pass fluttered into the arms of Cowboy defender Mel Renfro. Unitas got up slowly, his hand crossed over his chest, and he walked slowly off the field. A bone in his rib cage had been fractured, and he would not play any more today. On the sideline Earl Morrall, the goat of Super Bowl III, hastily started to throw a ball, warming up.

The Cowboys kicked to the Colts and Earl Morrall entered the game with the ball on the Colt 48. Immediately he began to make up for that disastrous Jet game. He tossed a pass to Eddie Hinton at the sideline for a 26-yard gain. He flipped another pass that Roy Jefferson caught at the 15 and carried to the 5. A personal foul moved the ball to the 2. On his first series of plays Earl Morrall seemed to be on his way to doing what he had failed to do for 30 minutes against the Jets in Super Bowl III: scoring a touchdown.

Yet, in this wild game, it was not to happen. Morrall sent Norm Bulaich thundering three times into the heart of the Doomsday Defense, and three times Dallas hurled him back. With fourth and two to go, only 21 seconds remaining in the half, Earl called time out. He went to the sideline and consulted with Colt head coach Don McCafferty, who had succeeded Don Shula. This was McCafferty's first year as a head coach and he made Mistake No. 4. The play to call was the field goal for the almost-certain three points. Instead McCafferty told Morrall to pass. Morrall went back to pass, threw to tight end Tom Mitchell—and missed. The Cowboys took over and a few moments later the disappointed Colts trudged off the field at the half, losing 13-6.

On the first play of the second half the Colts made Mistake No. 5. They bobbled the kickoff and the Cowboys pounced on the ball at the Colt 31. Tom Landry was sending each play in to Craig Morton on the lips of a "messenger" tight end—either Pettis Norman or Mike Ditka. Landry called for five running plays, and the Dallas runners—Duane Thomas and Walt Garrison—pounded down to the 2-yard line.

Now it was first down, two yards to go. If the Cowboys scored—and how could they miss?—they would lead 20-7. The game would be nearly out of reach of the Colts.

Mistake No. 6 would cost the Cowboys that seemingly certain victory. Duane Thomas took the ball from Craig Morton, sliced off left tackle, was hit at the line—and fumbled. A Colt jumped on top of the bouncing ball at the 1, and this sixth turnover had given the Colts a chance to come back.

Late in the third period, Earl Morrall was mixing passes and runs with a magician's slickness. The Colts moved to the Dallas 11. Earl stepped back, spotted Norm Bulaich circling in the end zone, and

Chuck Howley of the Cowboys, voted the game's most valuable player, makes one of his two interceptions of Colt passes.

threw. But Chuck Howley soared in front of Bulaich and intercepted for the Cowboys—his second interception of the day. Mistake No. 7 had cost the Colts the touchdown that could have tied the game. The score still was Dallas 13, Baltimore 6.

The Colts did not wilt. When they got the ball back, Morrall threw dart-like passes that moved the ball to the Dallas 39. In the huddle, on second down and a yard to go, Morrall called for the same flea-flicker play that he had botched up two years ago when he failed to see Jimmy Orr alone in the end zone.

This time he handed off to running back Sam Havrilak, who ran to his left, stopped and turned to flip the ball back to Morrall. But Sam couldn't: a big Dallas lineman had cut between himself and Earl.

The quick-thinking Havrilak turned, looked downfield and saw John Mackey open. He threw to Mackey. But in another strange play, Colt wide receiver Eddie Hinton veered in front of teammate Mackey, caught the pass and dashed for the end zone—past the 20, the 10. . . .

Naturally, in a game like this, he didn't score. Mel Renfro tackled Hinton from behind, sending him sprawling onto the ground at the 5. The ball hopped out of Hinton's arms and bounded toward the goal-line. Hinton, ankles held by Renfro, strained to grab the ball, which was hippity-hopping away from him like a rabbit.

The ball bounced into the end zone and kept on

bouncing—right through the end zone and out of it. The play was ruled a touchback and the ball was given to Dallas on its 20-yard line.

Mistake No. 8 had cost the Colts another chance to tie the game. The score was still Cowboys 13, Colts 6, and time seemed to be running out for the Colts.

But now, with some nine minutes left in the game, the Colts stopped making mistakes and the Cowboys resumed making mistakes. Mistake No. 9 got the Colts the tying touchdown. Craig Morton went back to pass at his 23-yard line. He threw too high to Walt Garrison and the ball was tipped by the Colts' Jim Duncan into the hands of Baltimore safetyman Rick Volk.

Rick gathered in the ball and scooted all the way to the Dallas 3-yard line. From there, doing everything right this time, the Colts slammed across, Tom Nowatzke diving into the end zone. Dallas led 13-12.

Young Jim O'Brien trotted onto the field, pulling his helmet over his long hair. He told himself to forget that bad kick that had been blocked in the second period. He watched Earl Morrall set down the ball. O'Brien stepped forward, kicked the ball, and it sailed over the crossbar. The score was tied 13-13. A smiling Jim ran off the field.

"Way to go, Lassie," one of the Colts yelled. Jim grinned.

Time ticked by, neither team able to score. If the score were still tied after the fourth period, the game

Colt linebacker Mike Curtis waits
for the ball to be snapped.

would go into sudden-death overtime—the first
team to score would be the winner.

Fewer than two minutes remained. The Cowboys
had the ball on their 27, second down and a seemingly hopeless 34 yards to go. Many spectators
thought they would call a running play to use up
time and go into overtime. In overtime the Cowboy
Doomsday Defense might force the Colts into another mistake that could win the game.

Instead, the Cowboys commited Mistake No. 10,

the one that ruined any chance for them to win. Morton went back to pass. He threw a high pass to halfback Dan Reeves, an aging veteran, on the right sideline. Reeves jumped for the pass, but not high enough. The ball glanced off his fingertips.

Waiting for the ball to come down was The Animal, Baltimore middle linebacker Mike Curtis. Mike hugged the ball to his chest and battled to the Cowboy 28 before he was buried under a horde of Cowboys.

"Get ready to go in, Jim," an assistant coach shouted to Jim O'Brien at the sideline. Hastily, nervously, Jim began to flex his kicking leg. Out on the field the Colts ran two plays into the line, maneuvering the ball squarely in front of the goal posts and running out the clock.

Jim O'Brien felt nerves tugging at his stomach. This was just like his dream: someone trying to kick a field goal in the closing moments to win Super Bowl V. That someone, he now realized, would be himself.

The ball was sitting on the Cowboy 25, third down and seven yards to go. With nine seconds remaining, the Colts called time out.

Jim knew he would be going into the game to try to kick the field goal that would win the game. He licked his lips, his nervousness showing. The veteran Jimmy Orr stood next to Jim. "Don't worry about it," Orr said to the rookie. "Even if you miss it, we'll beat 'em in the sudden death." Jim nodded. Orr had made him feel a little less nervous.

He ran onto the field. Earl Morrall met him. "Just kick it straight through, Jim," Earl said. "There's no wind—just kick it."

Again Jim nodded. The Colts lined up, center Tom Goode over the ball, Morrall kneeling at the 32. Suddenly the Cowboys yelled, "Time out! Time out!"

Morrall stood up. "They're trying to make you nervous," he said to Jim as they waited for play to resume. "Don't let it bother you."

"I'm used to it," Jim said with a weak grin. He had grown accustomed to defensive tackle Billy Ray Smith yelling at him during those Saturday "scream drills."

Now the Cowboys were screaming at him. "You won't blow this, rook, will you? Sure you will, sure you will . . ."

Jim stared over their heads. He was grateful now for those scream drills. None of the Cowboys yelled as loudly or as fiercely as Billy Ray Smith.

Play resumed. The two teams lined up. Center Tom Goode snapped the ball to Morrall. Immediately two Cowboy lineman leaped on Goode's back, using it as a springboard to jump high into the air to block the kick.

Morrall calmly placed down the ball at the 32-yard line. O'Brien took a step forward, head down, arms spread wide. He kept his eyes on the ball, held by Earl Morrall's finger. His right foot swung forward. He kicked the ball, meeting it cleanly.

The ball soared upward, above the straining fingers of the Cowboy linemen, curving slightly to the right. Jim looked up and saw the ball arching above the goal posts, maybe six feet to the inside of the right post.

Morrall and O'Brien jumped upward, hands high in the air, imitating the referee, who also held his hands high signalling a score. The kick was good. The Colts led 16-13.

There was time for a kickoff and one more play—and time for Mistake No. 11. Craig Morton stepped

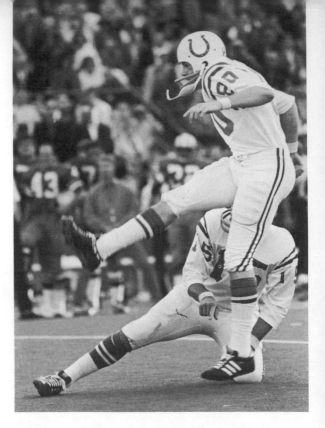

back to pass, threw another interception, and the
game was over. The Colts ran off 16-13 victors, winners of the Super Bowl in their second try.

The Cowboys walked slowly off the field. George
Andrie angrily ripped off his helmet and flung it at
the ground. The Cowboys had lost another big
game.

The Cowboys did win something. Al Silverman of
Sport was a surprise visitor to the loser's dressing
room. He gave linebacker Chuck Howley the keys to
the sports car for his two interceptions and all-
around tough defensive play. Chuck was the first

Jim O'Brien follows through on his last-seconds field
goal, watches the flight of the ball, then jumps for joy
as it flies between the uprights, giving Baltimore a
16–13 victory.

player who wasn't a quarterback to receive the Most
Valuable Player prize.

"If Duane Thomas hadn't fumbled on the one."
Tom Landry was saying in a corner of the dressing
room, "we would have been ahead 20-6 and in firm
control of the game. . . ."

In the winner's dressing room coach Don Mc-
Cafferty was talking about the two touchdowns that
the Colts had not scored because of Howley's inter-

ception and Hinton's fumble on the 2. "But the big play for us," McCafferty said, "was that interception by Mike Curtis that set up the field goal by O'Brien."

"Hey, Lassie," one of the Colts yelled at O'Brien. "I just took a survey of the players. You can keep your hair long."

Earl Morrall was sitting on a stool with a contented smile on his face. Johnny Unitas, his ribs aching, pointed at him and said to a reporter, "I'm so happy for the way Earl came in and did a good job. He was down after our last Super Bowl, but this made up for it."

Someone asked Earl how he felt. "The good memories always blot out the bad," he said with a grin.

Mike Curtis sat alone, thinking about the ring the Super Bowl winners get. That was what he had wanted. Not the money. The ring.

The Super Bowl ring. The ring of a champion.

SUPER BOWL V
(Played in Orange Bowl, Miami, Fla., January 17, 1971)

Scoring by quarter:

	1	2	3	4	Totals
Baltimore Colts	0	6	0	10	16
Dallas Cowboys	3	10	0	0	13

Scoring plays:

Team	Period	Elapsed Time	Scoring Plays	Colts	Cowboys
Cowboys	1	9:28	Clark, field goal (14)	0	3
Cowboys	2	0:08	Clark, field goal (30)	0	6
Colts	2	0:50	Mackey, 75-yd. pass from Unitas	6	6
Cowboys	2	7:07	Thomas, 7-yd. pass from Morton	6	12
			Clark, conversion (kick)	6	13
Colts	4	7:25	Nowatzke, 2-yd. run	12	13
			O'Brien, conversion (kick)	13	13
Colts	4	14:55	O'Brien, field goal (32)	16	13

Team Statistics

	Baltimore	Dallas
Total First Downs........	14	10
First Downs Rushing......	4	4
First Downs Passing......	6	5
First Downs by Penalty...	4	1

	Baltimore	Dallas
Rushes..............................	31	31
Yards Gained Rushing (net).....	69	102
Average Yards per Rush.........	2.2	3.3
Passes Attempted..................	25	26
Passes Completed...............	11	12
Had Intercepted...............	3	3
Times Tackled Attempting to Pass	0	2
Yards Lost Attempting to Pass....	0	14
Yards Gained Passing (net)......	260	113
Total Net Yardage................	329	215
Punts.............................	4	9
Average Distance Punts.........	41.5	41.9
Punt Returns.....................	5	3
Punt Return Yardage...........	12	9
Kickoff Returns..................	4	3
Kickoff Return Yardage.........	90	34
Yards Interceptions Returned......	57	22
Fumbles...........................	5	1
Opponents Fumbles Recovered...	1	3
Total Return Yardage............	159	65
Penalties........................	4	10
Yards Penalized................	31	133
Total Points Scored...............	16	13
Touchdowns...................	2	1
Touchdowns Running...........	1	0
Touchdowns Passing............	1	1
Extra Points..................	1	1
Field Goals Attempted..........	2	2
Field Goals Made..............	1	2
Total Offensive Plays.............	56	59
Average Gain per Offensive Play..	5.9	3.6

INDEX

Page numbers in italics refer to photographs.

169

About the Author

John Devaney is a free-lance author who specializes in sports. He is a contributing editor of *Sport* magazine and has written for *Boys' Life* and *Redbook*. He is the author of *Juan Marichal: Mr. Strikeout* and a book about the 1970–71 Milwaukee Bucks. Mr. Devaney lives in New York City with his wife and his sons, John and Luke.